"In *Tree of Lies* Scott Perkins writes about his own story with raw honesty and resolute hope – and seeks to help others who find themselves in that same place of wrestling. There are countless books on a myriad of topics, but few issues are as significant to write about as identity and faith. The questions Scott addresses are vitally important and his courage to face these issues head-on are admirable. Scott doesn't write from a place of ivory tower theory, but from the perspective of an in-the-trenches practitioner. If you want to address the issue of identity and purpose as it relate to life with Jesus, you'll find this to be a helpful tool for your journey."

—J.R. Briggs, Founder, Kairos Partnerships, National Director of the Epic Fail Pastors Conference, Author of *Fail: Finding Hope and Grace in the Midst of Ministry Failure*

"Tree of Lies is an authentic and transparent depiction of true struggles faced in today's church and society. People pleasing, burn-out and discontentment must be addressed to finally break free as believers and learn to live in the freedom that is offered through Our Lord Jesus Christ. This book is a great asset to anyone following Christ or feeling a call into ministry. You have to be real to be healed!"

—Mo Mydlo, Speaker and Bible Teacher, Author of *Overcoming Anxiety*

"I want more joy—don't you? The pursuit of joy can take us down a dead-end road when we invest our time and energy in the wrong things. In Tree of Lies, Scott Perkins gets to the root of the problem and sets you on a course to discover joy that lasts."

—Jim Akers, Founder of ImpACTful Notes, Author of *Tape Breakers*

"The Tree of Lies brings light to the way we all tend to craft a false identity, instead of looking to God to define us. This book inspires me, especially since Scott doesn't speak from a removed vantage point, but is vulnerable in sharing his own struggle with a faulty sense of identity. You'll be encouraged by the journey he will take you on!"

—Beth Steffaniak, Blogger at *MessyMarriage.com*, Marriage and Family Counselor, Life Coach

"Scott has masterfully depicted the challenges and struggles we face on our daily journey through this Powerful Book...A must read!"

—Joe Pici, Pici and Pici Inc., Author of *Sell Naked*

TREE OF LIES

Transforming Decisions,
Behaviors, and Relationships
By Gaining Perspective On
Your Identity in Christ

SCOTT PERKINS

AUTHOR ACADEMY elite

Published by Author Academy Elite
P.O. Box 43, Powell, OH 43035

Paperback ISBN-10: 1943526413
Paperback ISBN-13: 9781943526413

Hardcover ISBN-10: 1943526406
Hardcover ISBN-13: 9781943526406

Library of Congress Control Number: 2016909734

Author Academy Elite, Powell, OH

For Sarah.
Walk your path confidently knowing that you are approved of by Christ.
Stay aware of your root.
Follow Him wherever He leads.

Contents

Foreword by Kary Oberbrunner ix

Introduction: Not So Good Friday xi

PART 1: THE LIES

1 Burning Out: What was the problem? 3

2 The Tree of Life: What is identity? 17

PART 2: THE ROOT

3 The Root of the Problem: Where do
feelings of worthlessness come from? 33

4 The Cover Up: How does the false self work? 49

5 Core Lies: What is the story you tell yourself? 65

PART 3: THE TRUTH

6 God's Surprising Response to Brokenness:
Who is the God you are following? 81

7 The Desert Life: Who does God say you are? 95

8   Planting a New Root: What does it mean to deny yourself?   109

9   The Mystery of Faith: What is your cross?   121

10   Following Jesus: How do you develop a good root?   133

PART 4: THE FRUIT

11   Not Meant to Be Alone: How do you love others well?   149

12   Living Your Mission: What is your purpose?   163

13   Working It Out: How do you respond to failure?   173

Appendix A   Discovering Your Root   179

Appendix B   Developing an Identity Statement in Christ   181

Appendix C   31 Days of Identity Devotions   183

Selected Bibliography   185

Acknowledgements   189

Contacting Scott   191

Endnotes   193

Foreword

Our deepest wound is often the place where we'll have the deepest impact upon others. Our pain doesn't disqualify us. It makes us credible and believable.

None of us is perfect and yet some of us try to wear a mask and pretend otherwise. In *Tree of Lies* author Scott Perkins removes the mask. He shares his painful story of burnout that resulted while serving as a pastor. Because he overvalued relationships—to sustain his sense of worth—Scott abandoned his ministry and almost destroyed his marriage.

Tree of Lies is a breath of fresh air. It equips you to experience transformation in your decisions, behaviors, and relationships by:

- Developing awareness of areas where you are pursuing wholeness apart from God.

- Identifying the triggers and the lies that cause you shame.

- Creating a new mindset focused on the truth of who God is and who you are.

- Helping you get off the 'trying harder' cycle.

- Reducing busyness and anxiety.

- Identifying sources of conflict.

- Energizing and deepening your relationship with Christ.

- Beginning to live the purpose for which you were uniquely designed

Open up *Tree of Lies* and take the first step toward understanding your true identity in Christ. Once you know who you are and whose you are, you'll never be the same.

Kary Oberbrunner
CEO of Redeem the Day and Igniting Souls. Co-creator of Author Academy Elite.
Author of *Day Job to Dream Job*, *The Deeper Path*, and *Your Secret Name*

Introduction

Not So Good Friday

On Good Friday of 2009, I sat at the desk in my office of a large and fast growing church typing my letter of resignation. As part of my role as an associate pastor, I had performed a funeral the day before. While speaking words of comfort to several hundred people, I realized that I could no longer keep up pretending that my outside matched the inside. By all external measures I was successful. Internally, I felt disillusioned, insecure, and angry.

Very gradually, I had grown tired of trying to make my wife happy and I was frustrated with having to keep proving my worth at work. Feeling completely empty, I had just told my wife I was leaving her. I told her with a smile on my face. The next step was to resign my position at the church before anyone arrived at the office on this busy day.

This was not an act to get attention, but **my effort to find freedom**. You see, I had become something I swore would never happen to me. There was somebody in the church that I was going to start over with. If my wife wasn't willing to give me the closeness and intimacy that I thought I deserved, then maybe this new person would. If respect was going to be a carrot on a stick at work, then maybe what I craved would be found in a new situation.

So I abandoned everything.

Being a church leader, I had put on the mask of having everything figured out. I felt pressure to walk confidently in the way I followed Christ so others would know that choosing this path 'works.' I didn't want to be a bad example. Even with my friends, I didn't reveal too much. No one knew the depths of despair I felt about my marriage. I was in an unhealthy symbiosis with the people I worked with—I wanted to earn their approval, and it was given to me as a way to get me to work harder. Every day I felt off balance and insecure because I knew yesterday's accomplishments were in the past. For the most part, I put on a good face, hoping at some point I would get the security and wholeness that I craved.

The thing about it is, **when you wear a mask it is the mask that people are giving affirmation to.** Underneath, I was empty and exhausted. Conforming my behaviors to expectations and not allowing people to know me had left me without close relationships.

Even the couple times that I did reach out for help taught me negative lessons. On one occasion, I was told to try harder to be a good husband, and to put away the desires in my relationship with my wife. If only it were that easy.

On another occasion, when I confided in a friend, it led to some conflict about whether I was fit to be a leader in the church or not. So my mask was worn even tighter.

There is no effort on my part to blame others, for I walked into this situation willingly. I was reaping a reward. I was insecure and looking for people outside myself to affirm me and validate me.

When I gave everything up, my hope was that the insecurity and feeling spent that seemed to be such an ever present part of my life would finally go away. It came as quite a surprise that for the three months I was separated from my wife, things only got worse.

In my new relationship I was in constant conflict. A large part of the conflict was because of the demands that I was placing on it that I was oblivious to. I was making plans for a future that did not reflect what I felt the purpose of my life was. To top it all off, I also had doubts about whether God even cared about me anymore. More insecurity.

During this three-month period, I was literally afraid to die because I knew that everything I was doing was wrong. But in my mind, there was always the thought that if I can just get beyond this act of defiance, and show God how good I could be, then everything would be OK. Time plus good works equaled forgiveness. My mindset was completely focused on myself.

One afternoon, about three months after my not so Good Friday, I was driving in the slow lane on the highway, intentionally 10 miles an hour under the speed limit (remember, I was afraid to die), when I realized my effort to solve my own problem had gotten me nowhere closer to feeling complete. I started banging on the steering wheel in a rage and screamed at God, *"Why didn't this work? What do you want from me? Don't I get to ever feel happy?"*

The commonality to my situations before Good Friday and after was me. Without knowing it, I had brought the problem with me. Yes, my marriage was unsatisfying. Yes, I had surrounded myself with many unhealthy friendships. But the real problem was that I was using these things to form the root of who I was.

The insecurity, exhaustion, and anger were the fruit that I was experiencing because of where I had planted my root.

That day in the car, God spoke to me.

He said, *"It's your sin."*

Right away, I took this as a need to leave the new relationship and pursue reconciliation with my wife and church. Ironically, my first impulse was to focus on modifying my behavior. Of course that was necessary, but that was not the sin to which God was referring.

This was truly a miraculous turning point in my life. On that day, my eyes were open to examining my roots that were producing bad fruit. Fear, anxiety, frustration, impatience, anger, etc. are symptoms of a deeper problem. One that forms the core of who you are and who you think God is. Rather than avoiding the symptoms, trying harder to not exhibit them, or trying harder to produce good fruit, the response in Christ is to develop awareness of their source.

You cannot give it up until you have dug it up.

The aim of this book is to help you understand your roots and give space for Christ to transform your root and thus your fruit. In the pages that follow I'm going to let you in on my journey. I had set out to find freedom myself and I found true freedom in Christ. My hope is that you will allow God to lead you to the same thing.

Part One

The Lies

*I heard you in the garden, and I was afraid
because I was naked; so I hid.*

Genesis 3:10

As you work through this book, you can find a series of seven accompanying videos along with accompanying worksheets at **http://treeoflies.com/discover**. These complementary resources will help you identify areas that you are allowing to define your sense of self and begin to develop your true self in Christ.

1 | Burning Out

What was the problem?

As I sat in his office, the pastoral counselor repeated the question "On a scale of zero to ten, how empty are you in your relationship?" My first response was a lie. "I'm a five," I said. He didn't bite on my attempt to appear impervious because he laughed, and said, "What are you really?"

I sat in uncomfortable silence for a long moment, not being used to telling people the truth about my weakness. But since I was two thousand miles away from home with nothing to lose, I blurted out, "I am a big fat zero. There is nothing left in me, I'm totally spent."

The man on the other side of the room smiled, his reaction completely unexpected. Gently he asked, "Do you think God understands your emptiness?" Truth be told, I thought my emptiness was a disappointment to God. Having nothing left to give was a sign that I wasn't following Christ well enough.

"No," I said, "I don't feel like He does."

That was the moment my spiritual life in Christ changed direction.

For as long as I can remember, my life was about being good enough and attempting to earn the approval of others. No blame toward anyone is intended or implied with this statement. Even spiritually, following Jesus felt like running after someone who would not let me catch up. Regardless I was going to try as hard as I could to win the race.

What's more, I lived with the expectation that being good enough would produce good results. The principle of good fruit coming from my efforts may have some truth in some things. Still, it didn't hold weight for the majority of my life.

Despite my best efforts to be a good husband, I was not experiencing the married life I envisioned. My response to the lack of intimacy was to try harder to be a Christ-like example to my spouse, only to be disappointed when nothing changed for what I considered to be better.

At work I was continually on people's hook, filled with anxiety that I would let people down or experience a setback. There was no space for failure or weakness. Anytime I could prove my value I would, both to people of the church and those who oversaw what I did. I longed for approval and would go to great lengths to earn it. Regardless of what I had going on, there was always room on the schedule for one more thing. I wanted to be the solution to every problem.

As a dad I felt a nagging sense of inadequacy. My imperfect behaviors and decisions were going to be the cause of my daughter's brokenness. If only I could be a good enough dad, then I could save her a lot of trouble. Worry about how short I was falling motivated me. The idea that she has her own salvation to work out filled me with fear. I was never satisfied with how I was discipling her or that I was a good enough example of healthy masculinity.

With friends, I used my ability to ask questions and listen as a way to hide. Even with those whom I would have considered my closest friends I never revealed too much. In the moment it would not have occurred to me that this guardedness was an intentional strategy; it was important that it seemed like I had everything figured out.

My act extended to God as well. Unable to keep everything together, I felt like a disappointment. As if I was just one screw-up away from being written off by God. I could tell people about the love and grace that we receive in abundance through Christ, but those things were not a reality to me spiritually. I needed to be good enough for God's acceptance.

Not a pretty picture, right?

But maybe some parts of this sound familiar to you.

Looking back, I am saddened that I literally wore the clothes people expected me to wear, and that I allowed people to take advantage of me because their needs meant more than my own. I gradually moved further away from who Jesus created me to be. Instead of embracing my strengths and design, I became who people expected me to be so that I could get what I needed. As a result I was on the fast track toward burning out.

There was no possibility of rest in my world. Vacations filled me with dread. (What if people needed me and I was not there for them?) I would answer the phone at any time. (My work and personal boundaries became nonexistent.) Despite my good performance, I felt the things I did could always have been done better. Every task, every relationship necessitated proving my worthiness again. There was always something else to do and someone else to help. Simultaneously I was bound by people's expectations and the fear of failing to live up to them.

There was rarely peace. When you rely on others for a sense of approval, you begin to resent their need. That was true of me. People would come to me for help because it is what I offered. Even though I craved their approval, I was also filled with a growing resentment toward them as well.

I picked most of my personal relationships based on who could provide me the most emotional return. Subsequently, I made many bad choices in friends. Cheerleaders will cheer for you when things go well, but will disappear when you need them. When your relationship is symbiotically based upon performance, people will move on when you can't produce anymore. To top it all off, I extended compassion and tolerance to others, giving them the freedom to stumble and make mistakes, while denying myself those exact same things.

My relationship with God felt desolate. I thought I knew God's purpose for me. I thought I was pursuing it, but so often God seemed quiet and distant. It seemed impossible to be sure that I was on the right path. The circumstances of my life made me want to run away from my calling almost daily and left me questioning if I was doing what God wanted me to do.

My sense of being OK was tied to earning the approval and admiration of others and the Jesus that I was following was just another person who wanted something from me. Like with everyone else, my relationship with Him was filled with anxiety, insecurity, expectations, and exhaustion.

Afraid of Insignificance

All of this emptiness was the result of a lie; in fact, it was the LIE that has been around since the beginning. It was the original LIE that Adam and Eve fell for in the garden. This same LIE that Abram and Sarai succumbed to when Abram fathered Ishmael. Again and again, throughout the Bible, we see people fall for the LIE. We see it when David called for Bathsheba and when Peter denied his friend Jesus three times. In fact, it is this LIE that takes our freedom, rest, and pulls us off the narrow path.

Here is the central lie:

That you need something in addition to or in place of God for wholeness.

The enemy convinced the first man and first woman of this in the garden. That God was not enough. And throughout all of history it is this same LIE that has entrapped and disrupted the lives of the people living in this world.

Take the case of Abram as a typical example. God made a bold and miraculous promise that Abram was going to be the father of a multitude. This promise was to be the fruit of the relationship Abram and Sarai were enjoying with God. Yet, they started believing that more was necessary. The LIE was rearing its head. Having children became more important than the relationship with the God who gave the promise. Their actions and decisions that followed were the product of making something additional a requirement to feel accepted and significant.

In my own story, what I desired, in addition to a relationship with God was the approval of others. To be noticed, I sought and attempted to generate affirmation. God was not enough, my significance and sense of wholeness were tied up in feeling approved by others.

Yet, I am not alone. Look around at the people you know. Are those who lead your church experiencing the freedom and rest that Christ assured His followers would come from a relationship with Him? How about those in your small group? Your neighbors and family? Are you experiencing it in your own life?

Everyone is struggling with a passion for self.

We feel that extra attributes are necessary for us to feel secure and loved, which means that we think we have to add to the promise of Jesus. These extra attributes are standards the world lives by. People talk about wanting a relationship to make them feel complete; that priority will drive decision making. In churches this can take the form of adding burdensome expectations on how a follower of Christ should look and act. For others, it is being a good parent. Financial security, being heard, sexual conquest, health, political control, having the right body image, knowledge—and the list can go on and on. These are all things that we look for to supplement or substitute for our relationship with God.

At its core, this is a spiritual problem. At the beginning of the fourth chapter of his book, James taught:

> *What causes fights and quarrels among you? Don't they come from your desires that battle within you? You desire but do not have, so you kill. You covet but you cannot get what you want, so you quarrel and fight. You do not have because you do not ask God.*[1]

What you are experiencing is not new; James talked about the exact same struggles. The behaviors and decisions of the followers of Christ that James wrote about were influenced by their belief that something in addition to God was necessary for their wholeness. They were fighting and quarreling, coveting and comparing, battling within themselves the entire time and leaving God out of the picture.

The things you pursue steal your rest by convincing you to just try a little harder to provide for yourself. They ensnare and entrap by convincing you to work just a little harder, give a little more until you're left feeling worthless and spent. In your effort to build this part of life away from God, you will become focused on building your own kingdom rather than the kingdom of Christ.

Covering Up the Fruit

The disciple who lives trying to complete themselves outside of Christ produces bad fruit. The fruit of life consists of your decisions, behaviors, and the ways you relate to others. Bad fruit takes many forms, including:

- Enmeshed relationships

- Unending busyness

- Ineffective worry

- Constant anxiety

- Building resentment

- Unaddressed insecurity

- Exploding anger

- Justifying greed

- Seeking approval

- Numbing addictions

This fruit is inconsistent with one who is resting in God's love for them, and it creates a tension within your spirit. You begin to experience the exhaustion and isolation of the cover up. Many church systems have an unwritten rule: When you are in Christ, the redeemed life is "all fixed". Failure is not something to learn from; rather, it is something that should not exist. Struggling or stumbling is a sign of backsliding. Disappointment and longing are considered expressions of a lack of gratitude.

Few followers of Christ have the experience of being instantly and permanently fixed. Even the apostle Paul had a thorn in the flesh[2] and spoke of a battle to obey.[3] Certainly it is within the power of God to wipe everything away, but while your citizenship is in heaven, you are still present in this broken world. Spirituality is messy. Despite this truth, there is fear of telling a small group that somehow the relationship with the woman at the office has turned romantic. Or that you are overwhelmed with the needs of your kids. Or that when you think about the church or ministry you are leading, that you only feel secure and effective when the numbers are going up.

Around others, you are expected to put on the face that says everything is fine. Jesus is working in your life. If something doesn't go as you would like, you counsel yourself that God works all things for good for those who love Him. Meanwhile, underneath you are hurting and confused. Filled with questions about whether or not you are following Jesus the correct way because life still seems such a mess.

Even worse is when these questions cause people to give up on following Jesus all together. With a mindset of *"I tried that and it didn't work"* or *"there is no hope for me,"* off they go to fulfill themselves in a way that has more immediate or easier results. That is the place that I found myself in because everything I tried (and a lot of it was the *'right'* stuff) seemed to fail.

When I grew more and more desperate, I would ask God to write the answer to my prayers for direction in neon in the sky. That didn't happen and it only augmented my sense of distance from God. My feeling was that to be faithful to Jesus meant that I had to take my medicine and shut up.

The silence that your prayers are seemingly met with is frustrating and discouraging. But, from the James passage quoted earlier, a large portion of this seeming silence may come from your approach to prayer—taking to the task with the sense of wanting to accomplish something and checking it off the list. No one gives up control easily, even in prayer.

The bigger issue is the idea that you are asking with the wrong motive, but at the same time, have not honestly addressed what your motive is. Rather than being open to what the answer would be, you are simply asking God to bless and make prosper your pursuit of wholeness apart from Him. When God holds fast to His will being done, you interpret that or feel that as silence.

What Is the Problem?

The values and beliefs that you enter into Christ with and which form the basis for your decisions, behaviors, and ways of relating to others are broken. In your effort to create your own wholeness, you cling to these values and beliefs because they are comfortable and familiar. As you tire of the cover-up and let people in, you may be told by others to "just stop" doing what you are doing, or to "try harder" to make your choices align with Christ's example. Sometimes, the advice is spiritualized to say you simply need to "have more faith."

If only it were that easy.

Rather than being helpful, that well-intentioned advice simply compounds the frustration and inadequacy already present. While there is truth to saying that faith is important or that God works all things for the good of those who love Him[4], expressing that as the only solution is the spiritual equivalent of saying "suck it up and deal with it." In sports, the expression is "walk it off." The pain is still there, but the response should be to ignore it and keep playing the game.

Jesus promised His followers freedom[5] and rest[6]. Yet, the people I've met and coached, both those in churches and those who have given up on the church, seem to exhibit just the opposite fruit in their relationship with God. They are trying very hard to walk it off, similar to how I would not admit to my counselor that I was a zero on his scale.

When you are in this place of striving, there is little experience of freedom with others. Rather relationships are filled with resentment, jealousy, anger, blame, and unmet expectations. For most, the response to this unwanted fruit is self-protection. Covering up and presenting a safe version of yourself for another to see. Living in vulnerability and extending compassion seem like irresponsible concepts.

Freedom with God seems foreign. As circumstances challenge you, God bears the brunt of your blame. After all, if He sustains *all* things then shouldn't things be better in your marriage or with your health? Instead of freedom, there is doubt of His goodness. Grace seems a very distant concept. So much experience with God is bound by a false and unexamined understanding of who He is.

Finally, there is no freedom with self. Anxiety and insecurity are ever-present companions. Many followers want to be like someone else, to have the faith of the apostle Paul, for instance, rather than delighting in the particular strengths that God has given them. To walk the spiritual path of another by comparison is a trap. Fear, uncertainty, anger, and inadequacy are the opposite of freedom.

Not living in freedom, peace, and rest is an issue that must be addressed. Attempting to deal with it and walk it off is part of the pursuit of a wholeness independent from God. It is self-management, and what it really means is ignoring a problem that will become larger and more consuming the longer you wait to address it. Bad fruit is not, in and of itself, the problem. It is a symptom of a much deeper problem.

The first problem is lack of self-awareness of who you are and for what you are living. Developing such an awareness is not the same as pride. In fact, it is pride that keeps people from becoming aware of motivations and sources of significance.

It is impossible to release your grip on the false things you cling to if you do not understand why you are hanging on to them in the first place. Using a different analogy, it is hard to successfully fight an adversary you know nothing about.

So much of who you are has been shaped by relational systems that are broken. It is necessary to understand how that has impacted your view of who God is and how you view yourself.

If you are like me, you are believing lies about who God is and who you are. This false narrative that you tell yourself keeps you struggling on the same path, trying harder and harder to get what you need from relationships, roles, and possessions. None of these things were designed to sustain your sense of wholeness.

The other side of the problem is how you approach discipleship. Without a growing self-awareness, becoming a disciple will take the form of adding Jesus to who you already are. Things would be great if Jesus would just make you a better, more effective version of your present self. Without real change, your requests shift into asking for Jesus to bless your marriage, get the promotion or new job, find time to read the Bible, or any number of other things that don't require you to understand where your resistance to the will of God comes from.

Discipleship tends to be taught as "one size fits all." Follow these steps, pray this way, and be in the church building as often as possible. Settling for the spiritual version of self-improvement is easier and less messy than surrendering to God. It also allows you to maintain control.

The result is a life in Christ that is driven by *do, do, do*, as in the case of Martha when Jesus was visiting the home she shared with Mary.[7] Martha was driven to prove her worth and demonstrate that she had it all together. Simultaneously, she demanded that her sister Mary value the same thing. Martha was choosing a substitute that lacked the power to transform.

In just the same way, proving yourself to God adds more busyness to an already busy lifestyle. Maybe this is why so many people are choosing to avoid spiritual growth altogether[8]—it becomes just another thing to cram into life, and ultimately, what is produced is not worth the effort. An alternative would be to examine the root of why you are so busy in the first place.

As He responded to Martha's frustration, Jesus invited her to confront what she was clinging to for worthiness. He did the same thing in my life and He is calling you to the same thing in your own.

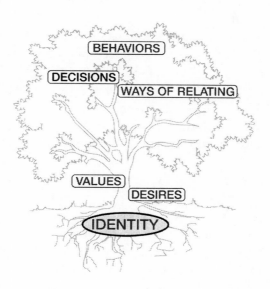

Figure 1 – The Identity Tree

The Root and the Fruit

Jesus taught: *"Make a tree good and its fruit will be good, or make a tree bad and its fruit will be bad, for a tree is recognized by its fruit."*

Here is the unfortunate response to this teaching: focusing on the fruit (see Figure 1 – The Identity Tree above). No matter how many times you pick an apple off the tree and clip an orange on to the branch, it remains an apple tree. Same goes for human beings; regardless of how hard you try to manufacture good fruit, i.e. doing good works and covering up the bad, if the tree of your life remains unchanged then all you are doing is presenting a fake version of who you are.

But what is impossible for people is possible for God.

It is impossible for a person to become more presentable to God under their own effort. What you consider good, done apart from Him, God considers filthy.[10] It is impossible for you to obtain the wholeness that you crave apart from the One in whose image you were created.

While it is important to be aware of your bad fruit, and while it is also important not to give yourself permission to do whatever you want, it will be impossible to "just stop" doing what is wrong and "try harder" to be good. Making a tree good does not happen by forcing the fruit to be good; instead, making a tree good happens by addressing the root of the tree.

If you want to develop good fruit, you must understand your root.

If you want to change your decisions, behaviors, or ways you relate to others, then you must address your source of significance. When you understand where your life is rooted versus where it should be rooted, the fruit of your life will be transformed.

From that encounter on the counselor's couch, I still had a long way to go, but something new was starting to take root.

What this book offers is the path to follow Jesus into His rest. You are about to embark on an examination of how to experience the freedom that you have been promised and follow boldly the unique and wonderful mission for which God has designed you.

This is a story of hope. It is a journey for anyone who is stuck and rooted in the wrong things, and for those who are exhausted from trying harder without progress, so they can begin to understand how to be rooted in the One thing.

And give God permission to take care of the rest.

Gain Perspective

- On a scale of 0 (never) to 10 (always), how would you rate your level of freedom and rest you are experiencing?

- How would you define wholeness or completeness of your life?

- What negative decisions, behaviors, and/or ways of relating are affecting your present life?

- In regard to the previous question, how effective have you been in 'just stopping' or 'trying harder'?

- What obstacles to connecting with God do you experience?

- What goals to you have in your relationship with God?

- Appendix B explains an exercise to help you develop an Identity Statement in Christ. Set aside some time and begin yours.

2

The Tree of Life

What is identity?

It is often possible to tell a little about someone by the stickers they have on the back of their car. Many windows have cute little stick figures representing the family. There are statements about who people are voting for, calls to coexist, information about a particular cause, expressions of values, and various logos for companies, clubs, and sports teams.

I myself have three things displayed on my rear window: a '13.1' sticker that lets people know that I am more athletic than I look, a Florida Gator logo to declare the superiority of my collegiate affiliation, and a cling that is the parking decal of the college for which I am an employee. All affixed in an effort to allow those following behind me in traffic to know me a little better.

There is a tendency we all have to send some sort of message to others about who we are. While you may not use the back window of your car, there are a multitude of other ways to communicate it. The type of clothing you wear sends a message, as does where you shop; the type of car that you drive; where you live; and the types of places where you spend your time at. Some of the messages are intentional, while some are not. Some are subtle, while others are crying to be noticed.

On social media you communicate accomplishment or pride through pictures, videos, and brief statements. All in an effort to get others to notice where you are, what you are doing, who you are with, and how you look. The likes and replies and the interaction bring with it a feeling of being noticed, accepted, and deemed significant.

Statements about what make you significant are also used to determine how you measure up. Your life may be like a leader board, and the statements that you hold onto for a sense of worth also allow you to determine if others are better or doing worse than you.

In my own life, I have a tendency to feel valuable when I am liked and noticed. In order to gain that sense of value, I will help others, listen diligently, defer my desires, and automatically blame myself for problems. For when others are happy with me, then I am happy with me.

One of the coaching clients that I have worked with feels a sense of worthiness when he is productive. At the end of each day, sometimes at the end of each hour or each task, he will judge his own worthiness by how much he has gotten done. Ask him to describe how he was and he would recount all that he had done so far that day. The task list that he kept with him was the indicator of whether he felt good or bad about himself and his relationships.

An increase or decrease in a sense of significance can be tied to almost anything. Parents can determine their own worthiness by how their kids behave. Have you ever watched the chagrin on parents' faces in a restaurant when their kids are being loud?

Pastors and church leaders I know evaluate the value and significance of their work based on size and growth.

Another client only saw herself as loveable and secure when in a physical relationship with a man.

Where you find significance is not limited to one area; rather, it can be multifaceted, or feel second nature to you. Relationship status or lack thereof may be tied to worth, as can be income, fitness level, sex, careers, sports, religious activity, amount of education, popularity, appearance, and so on.

The foundation of your sense of self is called *identity*. Your identity is your perception of what makes you valuable, loveable, worthy, or complete. It impacts how you relate to the world and how you interact in relationships. In and of itself, this quest for significance is not the problem; every person that is alive and has ever lived was created longing to be found valuable.

Created in the Image of God

In the story of the creation of mankind, we are told that the first man was formed from a pile of dirt into which God breathed life. But God saw that it was not good for man to be alone. In order to rectify the situation, the Creator took a rib from the side of man, and created a companion who was promptly named woman. It is interesting to note that it was not until the creation of the woman that God called everything he made not just 'good' but 'very good'. The special significance of relationships caused God to change His evaluation of everything He had made.

The overview of this event adds in a key detail: *"So God created mankind in his own image, in the image of God he created them; male and female he created them."*[1] Mankind was created in the image of God. The image of God was intended to be the core of our nature and being; making us human and distinct from the rest of God's creation. What gave the first man and woman, and you as well, a special place among the entire creation was that they were all formed to be in the image of God.

This image of God is the projection of his love, goodness, and magnificence unto those he created. Instead of living at the whim of the creation, mankind was to subdue it, tend it, and cultivate order out of the wilderness.

Living in the image, Adam and Eve knew the truth about who they were and to whom they belonged. It was clear where they came from and there was a certainty about the purpose they had and where they were going. This image was the source of identity. God was their source of value.

The creation itself was good and would submit to their hands. Adam and Eve were placed in the middle of a garden made just for them, which provided for both of their needs, as well as became a place of communion with the One who created them. Everything in their environment directed their attention the goodness, faithfulness, generosity, creativity, nurture and love of God.

The creation was a reminder of the source of their identity, rather than competition for it. Born in the image, the first couple would identify with the source of the image, not with the creation. Every created thing in the garden testified to whom they belonged.

Implications of Identity

From their identity flowed purpose. It was simple really, be fruitful, multiply and subdue the earth.[2] In this way they related to the world around them. Dominion and stewardship was their role in the world. Creating order out of the wilderness and seeing good results from their work. And if anything went wrong, their worth was not dependent upon their performance.

With nothing impeding the image of God, there was a perfect communion with Him. He walked with them in the garden and they recognized His voice. Having a relationship with the Creator was natural, without fear, and they trusted that He would not leave them nor forsake them. The man and his wife had a perfect sense of self, a clear purpose and place, and their source of value was secure and unchanging. God regarded them highly.

The man and woman knew how to relate to one another. Because their identity was rooted in the image of God, the first couple experienced security in relationship. Each of them reflected the image to the other, so there was no fear of letting the other down, or being inadequate. At the very end of the creation account, the last thing we are told, the last glimpse that we get of the perfect couple is that they were naked and felt no shame.[3] The feeling of shame is based in the fear of not being worthy of love or acceptance.[4] It is the feeling of worthlessness or of being found inadequate when measure against some standard.

The absence of shame is significant because it means there was no fear of being unloved or being unaccepted. Each knew and was confident that the other had their best interests at heart. Selfishness, using another to meet one's own relational needs, was not a part of their experience. Neither would be the idea of withholding from the other or manipulating the other to get what they wanted. Abandonment was not a fear; neither was rejection. There was not a sense that the other was going to see something that would cause the relationship to end. Thus, there was no constant impulse to try harder to be good enough or to hide from each other.

When we think of being naked, our minds might automatically rush to nakedness of form. Being in front of each other without clothes would cause no fear of rejection or not measuring up to expectations. This would certainly be true since the idea of the man and woman having a covering does not come about until later in the story.

Yet, the concept of nakedness actually goes far deeper than just the skin. They both lived in emotional nakedness. Without a fear of rejection, vulnerability with each other and with God would have been natural. Without anxiety, Adam and Eve could reveal themselves to each other and be fully known. Because neither was the basis of worth for the other, each would feel adequate in their roles, not being diminished by their inherent differences. Additionally, they did not feel burdened by the weight of sustaining another's sense of self.

Vulnerability necessitates that you must first know yourself. It is the ability to accept not only your strengths, but also your weaknesses and differences because your identity is not based on others' affirmations. Both of them knew they were crafted in the image of God with the expressed purpose to be fruitful and multiply and bring order to the creation laid out before them. The result was intimacy, which Adam poetically described as Eve being "bone of my bone, flesh of my flesh."[5]

Adam and Eve were not created to complete each other. Each was individually created to be complete in God. When Adam was alone, God determined to craft someone 'suitable' for him.[6] The word suitable has the seemingly contradictory meaning of 'like opposite'. Alike and opposite, they were created to complement one another.

Complementing does not mean enmeshed, a state in which at least one member of a relationship is dependent upon the other for a sense of self. Nor were they disassociated, approaching the relationship coolly to avoid losing independence. They were interconnected; separate yet distinct.

Each was their true self. Existing as God had designed, in His image. Neither attempted to get something they needed from the other person. Nor was there a compulsion to be what the other person expected.

Part of the beauty of the scene in the garden is that there was an absence of shame in their relationship with God. He was not seen as an adversary, instead He was given trust and intimacy. There was no distance between either of them and God, and it was clear that the One who created everything had their best interests at heart.

Identity also brought with it boundaries. In addition to purpose and the absence of shame, the fruit their God-formed identity was valuing what He valued. Not eating from the tree of knowledge of good and evil was not a burden to bear, but an expression of their true selves.

For the man and the woman, having the image of God as their source of value defined them and their relationship with the world around them. There were no self-protection strategies, no battles with self-esteem and no barriers to relationship. Love for God, each other, and self could be done well. Adam's desire was for Eve, and Eve's desire was for Adam. And both lived in relationship with the God of the universe.

Shame did not exist.

Outside the Garden

As the story of the Bible unfolds beyond the garden, we see God longing for the people He has created to see their source of self as His. Here are just a few examples.

Abram heard these words from God: *"I am God Almighty; walk before me faithfully and be blameless. Then I will make my covenant between me and you and will greatly increase your numbers."[7]* Rather than reading those words as a command for perfection (and hence something that sounds unattainable to your ears), hear them as an invitation from God.

God invited Abram to live a life in union with Him and in His image, instead of leaving Abram to walk on his own and try to create his own sense of worth. Like Adam and Eve, Abram's blamelessness was going to come from walking in an intimate relationship with God Almighty. Some specific fruit is promised from this relationship, but that is not what makes Abram significant. Identity was to come from being joined with God in His promise.

When the nation of Israel was being rescued from Egypt, God instructed Moses to tell the Israelites that he was claiming them as his people. *"I will take you as my own people, and I will be your God."[8]* The way this nation of people was to be defined was as the people of God. Their significance as a nation was not from being the largest or most powerful, but from being the nation covered in the goodness of the Creator of the universe. Part of the fruit of that identity would be a place that was prepared for them, a place that like Eden was flowing with milk and honey.

Just like the first couple, this identity as the people of the one true God would give the Israelites purpose and security. From the relationship they would not have to feel inferior to any other nation, but instead their existence would be a reminder to the world of who God was.

One attribute of being the people of God was that the Lord himself was going to be their King, unlike any of the other nations of the world. In the latter parts of those days, Samuel was the prophet speaking God's truth to the nation Israel. As a prophet,

Samuel was experiencing fellowship with the Father; his sense of self was rooted in being one of God's chosen.

When the Israelites wanted a human king in order to be just like all the other nations, Samuel was displeased, probably experiencing the shame of the decision that the Israelite elders were demanding. But, Samuel's identity in God acted as his shield. And the LORD told him: *"Listen to all that the people are saying to you; it is not you they have rejected, but they have rejected me as their king."*[9] Samuel's worth was protected and secure, for it was not him being rejected, it was the Lord that the Israelites distrusted wanted to be rid of.

Jesus walked the earth as the image of the invisible God.[10] This is the same image in which Adam and Eve were created. Christ came to redeem the brokenness of mankind and restore the freedom, rest, and purpose that was intended in Creation. Through Jesus, God has once again extended an invitation to humanity to experience union with him and find identity in His Truth.

The man Jesus was secure in his identity as the Son of God. He was affirmed in that identity the day that he was baptized. Crowds did not define him nor did the level of faithfulness of his disciples because Jesus knew to whom he belonged. Being fully man, Jesus experienced the same feelings and temptations that we struggle with on a daily basis. Yet, he was resolute that the Father was in him and he was in the Father.

From his identity came the purpose to redeem mankind, and it allowed Jesus to drink from the cup the Father had given him. Because of his identity, Jesus chose the will of the Father over his own. Obedience is the natural expression of an identity rooted in God.

Jesus described himself as the way, the truth, and the life.[11] The way to experience the invitation to loving union with the Father; the truth about who God is and who we were created to be; and the source of life.

Answering the Questions

Experiencing a true and fulfilling life is something that everyone dreams of. If you want to overcome the obstacles to peace and rest, then the journey starts with understanding your identity. Just as the roots of a tree are unseen yet vital to the quality of fruit the tree produces, so is identity essential to the type and quality of life that you will live. In order to grow as a follower of Jesus, you must understand what identity is and how it impacts your decisions, behaviors, and ways you relate to others and God.

As has been mentioned previously, your identity is what gives you a sense of significance, value, or of being loved. There are three questions that form the foundation of your identity. They are:

- What do you do?

- What do you have?

- What do people think of you?

What do you do? This is the question of control. You must be doing something in order to prove your worth. Doing is a way to actively create a sense of significance.

Think of how often and how easily this question rolls off the lips. In order to make casual conversation, it is likely the first thing that you ask someone upon first meeting them. This question forms the first impression that you have of someone. Think of how differently you would respond to or possibly pursue a further relationship with someone if they answered the question "What do you do?" with "I'm unemployed" versus "I run a multimillion dollar retail chain." Attributing more value to a person if they answer with the latter is judging by a standard of the world.

The western culture in which the audience of this book likely lives by is consumed with accomplishment and productivity. Significance is measured by how well time is 'spent'. If you were to tell someone you sleep eight hours every night, then they might deem you lazy or unmotivated.

Worth is found in doing.

One of my clients sought my help because he wanted to change jobs. It turned out that he was good at his present job and was having an impact with those he worked with and served. But there wasn't a sense of fulfillment. In his perception, and affirmed by those in his church who thought that what he was doing should be done on a church staff rather than in the business world, made him believe his effort wasn't good enough. His self-perception was being negatively affected by the question "What do you do?"

The equating of worth with doing even extends into the spiritual life, and may also be where this question is most dangerous. If you are doing more at church, or more community service, or engaged in more studying of the Bible, then that must mean you have a deeper relationship with God. Yet, this is not the basis by which Jesus measured the spiritual life.

What do you have? This is the question of security. A sense of self is defined and built by what is possessed and how it compares to what another has. What you have can be defined as objects, money, followers, knowledge, status, body type, or relationships—all of which can be used as a source of security.

One of the most common situations wherein I have encountered this question is in the realm of relationships. Many people see themselves as 'incomplete' if they do not have a significant other. This becomes the basis for judging worth: Finding value in a relationship, or lacking a sense of value outside of a relationship.

Church leaders are struggling because their worth is tied to how many followers, baptisms, and dollars they are bringing in. Successful ministry being determined by what the ministry leader has.

In our society, industries thrive because they take advantage of people's need to ascribe value in owning material possessions. Those who create new products—whether it is cars, clothes, or electronics—know that many, many people have their sense of self be related to what they have. So, for instance, you may ask someone where they live, what type of car they drive, or where they went on vacation all in an effort to see how you measure up. Significance coming from having more and/or better.

Many people find happiness in shopping. New clothes may make you feel better about yourself because they are fashionable and on trend. Yet, new clothes wear out, new phones get scratched, and then you are back where you started.

What do people think of you?[12] This is the identity based on acceptance. Deeming yourself worthy when people are happy with you.

The desire to be known and accepted goes back to the Creation story. The God who crafted mankind is himself a God of community, saying let us create man in our image.[13] The Father, Son, and Holy Spirit experience oneness with each other.

In the case of acceptance, your significance is reflected to you by those around you. This is called the reflected sense of self. As you look to others in order to provide a feeling of being loved, approved of, and affirmed, you are having a sense of self reflected to you.

The proverb *sticks and stones may break my bones, but names can never hurt me* will not be the case when you are dependent upon others' affirmation or agreement for a sense of rightness.

Who You Were Created to Be

In Athens, the apostle Paul had opportunity to present the meaning of the resurrection to the great thinkers of the day. The idea of the meaning of life was of great concern to the Athenians and they constantly presented new ideas on the topic.[14]

To the crowd of people and philosophers, Paul talked about the God who made the world and everything in it and also created nations with the hope that people would realize their need for Him.

In describing humanity's need for God, Paul quoted one of their own philosophers, saying it is because "in him we live and move and have our being".[15] Despite not know who God was, the Athenians knew the importance of knowing Him. God defines us and gives us purpose.

From God you derive your identity. You were designed to live and function and relate in the image of God. That is life.

Because Christ represents the fullness of God in visible, human form, all the questions of identity are answered completely.[16]

■ *What do you do?* In Christ it is not about what you do, but rather what Christ has done. Your worth not being based on performance is the source of your freedom and rest. Fruit is a result of the root means that doing comes from being.

- *What do you have?* In Christ you have everything that the Father can give you. All of His love, all of His grace, and all of His generosity are presented in the gift of Christ to the world. Because you brought nothing into the world and will be taking nothing out of it, your significance has nothing to do with possessions, followers, or anything else you would say you have.

- *What do people think of you?* This one is a little tougher to work though. In Christ you are fully loved and accepted. But people may reject you. In this, Christ is your shield. You are not experiencing the rejection or scorn because of who you are, but because of who Christ is. Very early in the book Acts the disciples celebrated being arrested because they followed Jesus.[17]

Because the answers to these questions of identity are dependent upon Christ, your worth is secure. Jesus is the covering for shame. Who you are will not change because of failure or weakness, but rather grace will continue to be given as you develop awareness of your root.

Being connected to the image of God allows you to be your true self; the self that you were created to be when God first thought of you. Having been created uniquely and intentionally, each of us is not alike in Christ. There are diverse temperaments, styles, talents, and gifts and each is important as another.

Your true self can only be found by being rooted in Christ.

The Tree of Life

Figure 2 shows the tree of life framework. This is the way that God designed all of us to function. The roots of the tree are the source of significance, wholeness, and worthiness.

Based on identity, values and desires provide the lens of what is right or wrong. Thus, values and desires will form the basis for why you will say yes or no to a decision, behavior, or relationship.

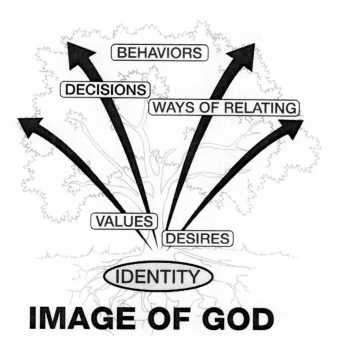

Figure 2 – The Tree of Life

Finally, there is the fruit of the tree of life. These are the decisions, behaviors, and ways of relating that are ultimately the product of the quest for identity. Jesus said that you will recognize a tree by its fruit because *good fruit comes from a good root.*[18]

Leaving the root of identity unaddressed leads to obstacles and frustrations in following Christ. If you are living with anxiety, poor spending decisions, insecurity, lust, anger, spiritual stagnation, unhealthy relationship decisions, unforgiveness, people-pleasing, etc., then you are struggling with a symptom of some part of your identity not being fully surrendered to Christ.

Being rooted in Christ (or some authors say centered in Christ) is not a role to play or a set of behaviors to adopt. Nor is Jesus an accessory to add to an already defined way of life. Clothed in Christ, you are hidden. The true self is a new self. By changing the root, your old self that clings to the familiar and comfortable answers to the questions of identity dies piece by piece.

Being in Christ means becoming more fully your true self. Then the fruit of your life will be an increasing expression of genuine love, joy, peace, patience, kindness, goodness, faithfulness, and self-control.

Gain Perspective

- What are some ways you see God's goodness in creation?

- How would your relationships be different in the absence of shame?

- Explain how God satisfied the needs for control, security, and affirmation for Adam and Eve.

- Which question resonates most with you? Why?

  » What do you do?

  » What do you have?

  » What do people think of you?

- Read Matthew 7:15-20. What bad fruit do you actively try to hide or overcome? What good fruit would take its place?

- Read Matthew 7:24-27, John 15:4-5, Galatians 3:26-27, and Colossians 2:10. What do these verses say about having identity in Christ? What verses can you add to the list?

Part Two

The Root

A good tree cannot bear bad fruit,
and a bad tree cannot bear good fruit.
Matthew 7:18

3

The Root of the Problem

Where do feelings of worthlessness come from?

It is virtually impossible to engage with any media today without encountering some advertisement for a new pill or miracle cure. Something that will make the bad go away so you can be happy. Facebook is littered with links claiming that "if you just eat this one super food" then you will lose weight or gain energy or solve some other problem. Television and magazines are no better, with every new drug having an advertisement boasting of miraculous weight loss, increased sexual prowess, or reduction of blood pressure. Almost universally, the people pictured are smiling and active and having no second thoughts at all about what was ailing them just a short time before.

The promise of happiness in one simple step.

In each case, these advertisements appeal to our desire to experience results quickly and without inconvenience. Taking a pill to lower blood pressure or decrease cholesterol allows the user to continue living how they have been, but no longer experience negative symptoms. There is the promise of a solution that allows you to avoid the decisions and behaviors that formed the root of the problem in the first place.

Emotionally, this has become the trend as well. A recently released study showed that over ten percent of Americans are taking some form of antidepressant. Again, allowing the user to be relieved of the negative results of depression, but potentially leaving unaddressed what is contributing to the problem. (I am not talking about clinical depression due to chemical imbalance here. Also, I'm not suggesting depression should not be treated.)

Whether it is a drug, supplement, or new, exotic super food, the intent of these treatments is to remove the experience of negative symptoms. Each is a way to manage an unwanted result without addressing the problem that created the warning sign in the first place.

When the symptoms go unheeded, the root of the problem will grow worse and worse.

Spiritual problems are treated in exactly the same way. Such was the case with my own spiritual life. I would ask God to "fix" my wife, but my motivation was so that I could get what I wanted. I wanted a miraculous intervention that would enable me to continue avoiding the reasons why I was so dependent on affirmation. That was the pill I was seeking.

Another strategy I would employ was to look for opportunities to speak or preach. The positive was that this was an activity I felt God had designed me for, and I wanted to grow my ability. But what I failed to address was how much I craved the approval and positive reaction of my audience. Their response was a quick jolt that allowed me to have the sense of feeling OK. On the off chance that I wasn't selected to speak, I would be left wondering why I wasn't considered good enough, rather than celebrate those who were given the opportunity to preach.

When things were going the way I wanted, I felt that God and I were close and doing well. When there was struggle, which was far more common, I felt a sense of desolation—God's apparent absence. My sense of self and the status of my relationship with God were dependent upon my circumstances and the fruit of my efforts.

I once met with a couple who came in my office to talk about their grown son who was living with them and sadly, also abusing drugs. They found out he had been stealing from them, which made them wonder what was going on. So they came to me and asked what they should do. The orientation of their question was not directed at allowing their son to feel the pain of his behavior, or to address why they were enabling him in the things that he was doing.

Instead, they wanted to know how they could fix him or get God to fix him, preferably with no one finding out. That was the solution their sense of self needed. In their case, identity was equated with being good parents, so fixing their son's behavior would make them feel worthy.

In the Bible, a young man approached Jesus and asked a straightforward question: What was the one thing that he could do in order to inherit eternal life?[1] In other words, he wanted a quick guarantee—the spiritual pill that he could take in order to get the sense of worth and wholeness that he desired.

Jesus' response made it clear that the young man only wanted a solution without addressing the problem. When Jesus instructed him to confront the power wealth had over his sense of self, the man went away sad.[2] With this one question, Jesus exposed the root of this man's identity.

Unhealthy fruit comes from having a poor root. Anxiety, busyness, poor boundaries, bitterness, lack of generosity, lust, etc. are the product of trying to find a sense of wholeness apart from God, becoming centered in self instead. This is the idea of the false self or what the apostle Paul calls the *flesh*.[3]

One time, a woman who was racked with anxiety came to see me in my office. Her to-do list was like a giant intimidating wall in front of her, casting a shadow on her entire day. Her initial question to me was, *"How do I stop feeling so anxious?"* As we talked, she was not interested in figuring out why she kept her schedule so packed to the brim. Her eyes were fixated on the symptoms. It had not occurred to her to look at the benefits she was getting from being so busy. All she really wanted was to have a new organizational technique or behavior that would make her more productive.

It is seemingly easier, and leaves us in control, when we attempt to address the problems rather than what is happening below the surface.

In the heat of the midday sun, Jesus conversed with a woman as she was gathering water at a well. Engaging in this chore during the height of the day's heat indicated that she was an outcast hoping to avoid the stares and gossip of others. As He engaged her in conversation He mentioned that if she knew to whom she was talking she would've asked him for living waters to drink. This woman, who was trying so hard to create her own sense of wholeness through relationships, turned to Jesus and asked for the water to be given to her so that she would not have to come out to the well anymore.

Her concern was in not having to worry about the well, the heat, and being confronted by others. She had missed the intent of Jesus' message because she was focused on a quick one-time solution. She wanted to keep living the same way, but get different results.[4]

In order to get relief from the spiritual exhaustion, loneliness, and feelings of worthlessness, we ask God to bless our brokenness. As we seek wholeness apart from Him, we simultaneously ask for better results.

In the last chapter, the case was made that our true identity and sense of worth comes from God. So, where are these symptoms and problems coming from and why are we so intent to solve them quickly?

The Challenge to Identity

There was one thing God had asked the man and the woman not to do. It was a boundary that when kept would demonstrate obedience. Obeying provided a way to express gratitude and trust in the Giver of life. Adam and Eve were not to eat from the tree of the knowledge of good and evil, or the promised consequence was described as death.[5]

Obedience is not oppression by God. Freedom always comes with boundaries. Adhering to this command was not a prerequisite for God's acceptance; it was to be the fruit of the relationship.

In the garden scene, a new character appeared. Something had existed that did not reflect the goodness of God to the man and woman. In fact, this serpent would spread a lie. He would tell the woman that God had held back on them, that there was something else they were lacking if they were going to be complete.

The serpent convinced the man and the woman that something else apart from God was necessary for their wholeness. This is the origin of the Lie.

Rather than being met with truth, the Lie was met with acceptance.

When they turned their attention to something else as a source of value, they broke communion with the Father. Their eyes turned from the image in which they were created to something that was created. Their first sin was breaking connection with God.

Disobedience is the fruit of that disconnection. With connection to the image now broken, they needed a new basis for their sense of significance.

The serpent called the worth and dignity of the man and the woman into question. By communicating that God was keeping something from them, he intimated that maybe they were not as special as God had indicated. Ultimately, the snake called into question the trustworthiness of God.

Because the source of their identity had been lost, the result was shame. Feeling worthless and questioning who they were was a new experience. The serpent promised glory and wholeness, but the result was fear and confusion.

Finding a sense of worth apart from God as a response to shame is the root of the problem. The broken image led to the man and the woman acting for themselves. Rather than being centered in God, they were centered in *self*. David Benner writes, "Everything that is false about us arises from our belief that our deepest happiness will come from living life our way, not God's way."[6] Pride is passion for self, and the result is a false sense of self.

The False Self

The three questions of identity form the foundation on which false identity is constructed: "What do I do?", "What do I have?", and "What do people think of me?" Whereas the true self is rooted in the image of God, the false self seeks answers in what was created.

There are three areas in which identity is defined apart from God and all were present in the experience of the first couple.

- Things

- Roles

- Relationships

Once Eve's eyes were fixated on the fruit of tree, she began to see how it could provide to her benefit. It was good for food, pleasing to look at, and desirable for wisdom.[7] Eve deemed that having the fruit would increase her significance.

When God came and expressed His disappointment, He let the man and woman know what the consequences would be. For their roles, the consequence was that they would look to them for value, but not be satisfied. Work was now going to be toil. Finding satisfaction in working was not going to be easy. The creation was now going to fight back.

One unique thing the woman had was her ability to bring forth life. In this role, God said there would now be pain.[8] Physical pain and the pain of disappointment. Children were not going to redeem her sense of shame, even though that is a place she would look.

Immediately after biting into the fruit, the man and the woman looked to each other for a sense of assurance, but were overcome by inadequacy. Before breaking connection with God, the relationship that the man and woman had was one of acceptance and blessing as each reflected God's image.

Afterward, they did not see that image fully reflected. There was doubt. The relationship was now a burden as they felt the weight of expectations that they could not fulfill for the other. God stated the depth of this burden to Eve.[9]

Relationships were not meant to bear the weight of another's identity. Neither, in fact, were roles or things created with the intent to make us feel significant.

The fall resulted from settling for less. Rather than experience their true self in the image of God, the man and the woman chose to pursue wholeness apart from him. The bedrock sin of the garden was not eating the fruit—it was the disconnection from the Author of life that preceded the mistake.

They believed the Lie and chose self over God.

The quick fix that Adam and Eve took in order to avoid the symptom of shame was to cover up and hide among the trees.[10] Much more will be said about this in the next chapter.

The Thirsty Root

The condition of Adam and Eve became the condition of everyone that followed them. When God addressed his people the Israelites through the prophet Jeremiah, here is how He expressed it:

> *"My people have committed two sins:*
> *They have forsaken me,*
> *   the spring of living water,*
> *and have dug their own cisterns,*
> *   broken cisterns that cannot hold water."*[11]

First, the people of God had forsaken him; they had forgotten to whom they belonged and in whom their identity rested. The roots of the tree of life are thirsty for significance, worth, and wholeness. God describes himself as the source of living water—water that will satisfy and strengthen the tree and bring forth good fruit.

The Israelites were choosing to believe the Lie and create their own source of wholeness. Through the passage in Jeremiah, God reveals the problem. The realization that must be contended with is that try as hard as you might, you will not be enough. The cisterns we dig, which are the places that we look for life and wholeness, will need continual filling.

Shame will keep rearing its ugly head. The tree of life will thirst.

This is why I got burnout from trying to sustain myself with approval and affirmation. No matter how much I got, the effects eventually diminished until more proof and validation of my worth became necessary.

From the examples mentioned at the beginning of the chapter, this explains why the parents needed their son to prove they were good. It is the same reason the young man who approached Jesus, despite being wealthy and claiming to have kept all the commandments, still needed something more. Anxiety plagued the woman in my office because her sense of worthiness was completely rooted in being perceived as productive. Being a broken cistern is why the woman at the well was on her fifth husband and still had unquenched thirst.

Apart from God, with your identity rooted elsewhere, your life will be dominated by a quest for worth. Within your soul you thirst for wholeness; that is what you were designed for. Even though it is a wholeness only God can provide, pride keeps you racing after the Lie.

Please understand that there is nothing wrong with feeling good about or experiencing delight in a relationship. Joy and love is what relationships were created for. Nor is it a sin to feel accomplished in what you do, for you were created for a purpose. It is not bad to have things and receive gifts. God himself delights in giving gifts to those he loves.

What is wrong is turning good things into ultimate things in order to feel worthy. When you make something into an ultimate source of value—whether it is a relationship, sexuality, political party, job, picture of an ideal life, retirement age, parenting style, and so on—you have created what the Bible calls an *idol*.

Idols become the ground that identity is rooted in, and they must be served. There is a constant list of demands from your idols—do better and do more. Worship is the act of finding value in something, the act of surrendering your sense of self to it.

Here's a major problem with your idols: they do not provide grace nor forgiveness. Either you meet the demands of the idol in order to get what you depend upon, or you don't. There is no in between. When you don't, in the absence of perceived value, shame returns.

As a sample example, I was coaching a woman who was also beginning to change her eating lifestyle in an effort to get healthy. Developing a healthier lifestyle is a great decision. What was robbing her of joy as she lost weight and became more fit was that being obedient to the new lifestyle became how she evaluated her worth.

She carried fear around with her, afraid that she was going to make a mistake or not adhere perfectly to her plan. If she was at a birthday party and decided to have a piece of cake, she was plagued by guilt and would say, *"I am so bad."* The good thing so easily became the ultimate thing, and not living up to the expectations of rightness that the idol demanded. She felt like a failure and would redouble her efforts to do better.

Abram and Sarai were promised a good thing. As a fruit of walking in the image of God, their descendants would be as numerous as the stars in the sky. Yet, even for them, the good thing became the ultimate thing and they judged their worth by the number of heirs they had produced: zero. Both of them began to serve this false source of worthiness.

While I was on staff at a large and fast growing church, a friend of mine once said that I just needed to stop caring what people thought of me. We both laughed and I affirmed that he was right, but I had no idea what to do about it. My wife was not able to provide me enough approval, so I turned my attention to getting it from my coworkers and members of my church. Relationships, something God had created to be good, had become the ultimate way I perceived myself.

In his writings, the apostle Paul often refers to the way that people define themselves apart from God. He called it serving the flesh.

"The acts of the flesh are obvious: sexual immorality, impurity and debauchery; idolatry and witchcraft; hatred, discord, jealousy, fits of rage, selfish ambition, dissensions, factions

and envy; drunkenness, orgies, and the like. I warn you, as I did before, that those who live like this will not inherit the kingdom of God."[12]

Each of these acts are completely centered in self, regardless of cost or consequence. Sex without commitment proves desirability. Hatred results from being kept from what is desired. Jealousy when others get what you want. Drunkenness numbs the pain of shame.

Regular conflict in a relationship results from one or both people relying on the other for a sense of self. When expectations are not met, or one is not getting what they need, anger, jealousy, or withdrawal ensue. Knowing that these things are wrong, there will be an effort to 'try harder' to earn the needed love or 'just stop' demanding so much.

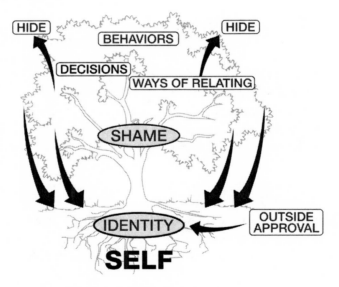

Figure 3 – Feeding the Root

People living like this will fail to inherit the kingdom of God because they are defining themselves apart from God. When centered in self and dependent on another source of value, the bad fruit will be clear.

Ultimately, that bad fruit of the false self is produced as a way to build up your identity apart from God. Figure 3 above illustrates how the false self operates. Decisions, behaviors, and relationships become necessary to prove your worth or provide the sense of wholeness that validates your identity. Bad fruit is hidden and outside approval is sought to further affirm the self. All of this is to cover the shame that is at the heart of being disconnected from the image of God.

Good Tree, Good Root

Jesus compared the lives and identities of the people he created to fruit trees in Matthew. Here's what he said:

> *"Likewise, every good tree bears good fruit, but a bad tree bears bad fruit. A good tree cannot bear bad fruit, and a bad tree cannot bear good fruit."*[13]

Notice that Jesus highlighted how there is a consistency between the type of tree and the fruit that is produced. Good tree produces good fruit. Bad tree produces bad fruit.

Understanding the concept of causation is the first key to developing an identity in Christ. This means that it is not bad fruit that makes the tree bad, and it is not good fruit that makes the tree good. You were created to bear fruit that is consistent with the root of your identity.

Bad fruit is the symptom of a misplaced identity.

The words of Jesus above cause a lot of confusion. When you experience relationship conflict, or struggle with lust, or are consumed with disappointment, instead of looking at what is making the tree bad, your focus is on the fruit.

Instead of growing closer to God in relationship, discipleship becomes a process of *managing* the decisions, behaviors, and ways you relate to others that the false self produces. As figure 3 illustrates, apart from God it is your decisions, behaviors, and relationships that determine how you feel about yourself.

Managing your fruit is done in two ways. First, you 'try harder' to produce good fruit because you want to be a good tree. Second, you force yourself to 'just stop' by hiding or ignoring decisions, behaviors, and ways of relating that you do not like or do not fit the image you are trying to portray.

In my own life, as I was rooted in peoples' opinions and perception of me, I would try to increase my sense of significance by being a person people approved of—being seen as a good follower of Jesus, a loving husband, and an attentive father. These were the masks that I would allow people to see.

At the same time, I battled the shame that came with having a dependence on outside approval. This meant that I was simultaneously trying to earn approval and to stop caring whether people approved of me. I was serving two masters.

I had created an image of what a good disciple looked like and I was conforming myself into that image in an effort to feed my false sense of worth.

I was managing my fruit and asking Jesus to bless the efforts of my false self.

A woman I coached was consumed with trying to become a "Proverbs thirty-one wife." In case you do not know what that refers to, the last half of Proverbs chapter thirty-one lists the attributes of a wife of noble character. Instead of seeing these as the fruit of the life that is rooted in the image of God, my client viewed this chapter as a checklist of behaviors to which she must conform in order to be a wife worth loving. Many of our conversations dealt with her sense of inadequacy at meeting that standard. She was trying to make the fruit good in order to make the tree good.

Similarly, in parenting we have this idea to raise our children in the way they should go.[14] Having obedient, well-behaved kids becomes the measure of whether you are good or not.

In the end, when you fall short and cannot manage to create a lasting sense of significance, when you become exhausted from the continuous work it takes to sustain a sense of self apart from God, you ask to have Jesus make things better. Without understanding the root of your identity, this step amounts to trying to add Jesus to who you already are.

Jesus is more than a cure for the painful symptoms of your life. He is not a pill to swallow that makes everything better.

Jesus did not come to help you better manage your behavior or help you perfect your old self; he came to make you a new creation by giving you a new root. In Christ you have been restored into fellowship with God and you can walk in His image.

Developing Awareness

Jesus told a story about a man who owned a vineyard on which a fig tree grew. Sadly, the fig tree had produced no fruit. When prompted to cut down the tree, the man who tended the vineyard refused to do so.

"'Sir,' the man replied, 'leave it alone for one more year, and I'll dig around it and fertilize it.'"[15]

Instead of focusing on the lack of fruit, the proposed solution was to address the root of the tree. **In order to change the fruit, you must focus on the root.**

Overcoming the false self requires an interior journey. Examining yourself in this way is difficult and compels intentionality. When examining your inward self, you may be confronted with difficult things that you may not like and that necessitates taking the brave and possibly painful step of releasing things that you have allowed to define you in order to provide a sense of worth.

There is fear and misunderstanding about beginning this process. Doesn't the Bible say that you should deny yourself? Doesn't that mean that you should avoid the inward journey because it is a focus on yourself?

Indeed, Jesus does tell you to deny yourself, and this will be the focus of chapter eight. But denial does not mean to ignore or avoid. Too often we confuse the act of denying with repressing or stuffing away so no one can see.

But God sees what is inside a person.[16] Without examining inward, it is impossible to deny your false sense of self.

Ignorance is not bliss.

Pride is putting yourself in the place of God; the inward journey seeks to find out what you have substituted for God so it can be confronted, have the light of truth shone on it, and be put to death. It is impossible to fight an adversary that you know nothing about.

Before I became aware of what identity was, ignorance was my reason for lack of peace and the cause of my spiritual exhaustion and emotional burnout.

I quit my job. I left my wife. And I blamed God for not working things out. I did not know what emptiness I was trying to fill, and simultaneously, what areas of my identity I was withholding from Jesus. Instead, I was adding Jesus-like behaviors to the person that I had already created. For many years, I was following Jesus on my own terms, not giving myself fully to him.

Part of this is the normal process of becoming a disciple. You will encounter God, begin to learn truth and what being a disciple is, and then become productive in your spiritual community.[17] This is a good start. But if the process ends here, which it does for so many, then religious performance will become another way to validate the false sense of self.

A discipleship based on *doing* is comfortable because it gives you the ability to prove your worth. The flip side of this is the insecurity or feeling that your 'faith' is not working when what you are doing lets you down. Like my experience, it will be living for a Jesus that you can control and which does not require too much of you.

Everywhere I go, I see this same pattern. With clients and those I have attended church with, the common perception is that by attaching more Christ-like behaviors to themselves then there will be the experience of being 'all fixed' and complete. When that does not bring the desired results, God's presence and love is questioned, or the whole Jesus thing is given up altogether.

The obstacle to spiritual growth and having a sense of the presence of God is asking God to make something work that was not meant to bear the weight of identity; it will not bring peace, rest, and purpose.

Before you can grow spiritually as a disciple and move beyond the strategy of trying harder, you must develop awareness of where your identity is rooted. It is necessary to see how you are answering the questions *what do you do*, *what do you have*, and *what do people think of you* outside of the image of God. Only when you begin to take a good look at your root will change begin to happen at the core of who you are. Rather than sustaining your false self, you will be developing your true self in Christ.

Developing an identity in Christ is about rejecting the Lie and surrendering to Truth. It is about centering your sense of worth and significance in who God is, and understanding who your true self was meant to be. It is about changing the way you think about yourself, God, and others. This is how Jesus will transform your life.

Gain Perspective

- Explain the Lie that the serpent used to challenge Eve's identity.

- Read Mark 2:21-22. Discuss how this passage relates to the idea of identity and understanding where it is rooted.

- Read Mark 10:17-23.

  » Put yourself in this man's shoes, why are you disappointed?

  » How does this relate to your own experience with Jesus?

  » In what ways would you describe yourself as 'rich' apart from God?

- What areas do you look to for wholeness apart from God?

- List the ways and situations you answer the three questions of identity in order to build your own sense of value.

- In your own life, how are you expecting Jesus to be a quick fix?

4

The Cover Up

How does the false self work?

In the coaching process, it usually takes a few sessions working with someone before they begin to feel comfortable enough to reveal some of the sources of worth that they hold close to themselves. Such was the case when one of my clients confided that he struggled with pornography.

He and his wife were confronting some issues, and one of them was her refusal to engage in a sexual relationship. Around the same time, he happened to see some pictures online—at first they were just pictures of women in bathing suits on a travel website. Then it became a search for women dressed in lingerie. After that it went much further.

As he related how he was caught off guard, he told me that it was their eyes looking at the camera and the smiles on their faces that seemed to be an invitation. While a part of him knew what he was doing was wrong and devalued his marriage, his justification was that since his wife wouldn't have sex with him it made what he was doing not as bad. He felt entitled to the pictures of naked women and his fantasies.

Disconnected from God, the false sense of identity is deceitful and destructive.

I present the story not to excuse his behavior, but as an example of how when we are disconnected from the image of God, decisions begin to be made by what is right in our own eyes. Each spouse is responsible for their own decisions and behaviors, which are the fruit of where identity is rooted. This client saw a part of his value as his sexual desirability, and it became easy to do what was right to support that sense of self.

Judas Iscariot was one of the twelve men who responded to Jesus' invitation to follow Him. For most of three years, Judas went where Jesus did and learned at the feet of the Rabbi. Yet, because Judas' worth was firmly rooted in being part of the political liberation of Israel, he was able to make the decision to betray the location of Jesus, which led to His arrest. Whether it was to prompt Jesus to action or simply for greed and the promise of power, Judas did what was right in his own eyes.

My own experience displays a similar pattern. I had tried everything I know of in order to win my wife's approval. My thought being, if I was just a good enough husband then I could make her happy. Because the root of my identity was not immersed in Christ, I became emptier and emptier trying to be her source of happiness, and eventually reached the point where I felt like I had nothing left to give. I was done, and the choices I began to make were those that I felt I needed in order to feel a sense of worth. It is unwise to use yourself to judge what is right and wrong for you.[1]

I began to pursue another relationship, which I rationalized was from God because it was making me feel noticed and whole. I also chose to abandon my calling. Becoming a pastor was something for which God had formed me. Yet, I quit my job because the role was going to impede my new pursuit. The Lie takes root with the promise of fulfillment, but provides disappointment and hardship.

Doing What Is Right In Your Own Eyes

Have you ever wondered how it is possible that your stated values can be completely ignored and you can create justifications for just about any decision?

Pursuing wholeness apart from God leads to doing what is right in your own eyes. Right or wrong being determined, not by some unchanging standard, but by what brings a sense of fulfillment and significance. Disconnected from the image of God, desires turn to how the false sense of self can be validated.[2]

Continuing the example from the previous chapter, Abram and Sarai had made the subtle transition of the root of their identity from the God who gave them the promise to the promise itself. Drawing significance from the promised multitudes of descendants, yet having no child, their values adapted to sustain the sense of self apart from God.

Because of the pressing importance of having a son, each year that went by highlighted their sense of failure. To cover their shame, Abram and Sarai agreed that Abram would have a child with Sarai's servant. This was not the plan of God. Rather, this was two people doing what they estimated was right. What's more, they then asked God to bless the result.

The Response to Shame

All of us can see our pattern of thinking in the example of Abram and Sarai. And as happens with all lies from the beginning, it did not live up to the billing.

After believing the Lie that something more than God was necessary to be satisfied, Eve looked at the fruit of the tree in a new way. She saw that it would satisfy the hunger of her new emptiness without God; that the fruit was also beautiful and offered her new wisdom.[3] These are the values of the false self.

After both ate the fruit and fully committed to the Lie, the man and woman were no longer reflecting the acceptance of God to one another. With that missing they responded to their shame for the first time. There was suspicion. Where there was once trust, there now existed fear.

In our modern day shame has become the topic of much research and writing. One of the leaders in this effort is a researcher named Brenée Brown. In her book, *I Thought It Was Just Me*, Dr.

Brown describes the shame response. How we respond to shame is the impulse that we go through when confronted with the feeling of not being worthy of love or acceptance.

In her book, she focuses two facets of the shame response: fight and flight. From my experience, I would add "the tendency to freeze."

Covering shame with the **fight response** is the effort to try harder, telling yourself to just stop, or to have more faith. This is the process of managing the fruit of your tree of life. By trying harder to earn love or to prove you are worth loving, you are doubling down on finding significance from false sources.

The **flight response** is trying to run away from shame. This can be done by hiding unhealthy decisions, behaviors, or ways of relating to others. A great example of this is the idea of blaming. When confronted by feelings of being worthless or feeling unlovable, one strategy of the false self is to blame circumstance or heap fault on another person's behavior.

In her June 2010 Ted talk on the topic, Dr. Brown defines blame as a way to discharge pain and discomfort. All of us are guilty of blaming. Saying words like *"I would have done it, but you…"* or *"It's not my fault, he…"* are examples of transferring fault. By placing blame on the shoulders of another, you are able to protect your sense of rightness.

Alternatively, the flight response can mean replacing one source of value with another. This was my own strategy. After trying so long to get validation from my wife, and failing, I turned my attention to immersing myself more fully in my role as pastor. Doing that provided a quick and easy boost to my sense of worthiness.

The final way of dealing with shame is the **freeze response**. When you freeze, you simply accept that you are without value or don't deserve love or forgiveness. Acting out of being frozen in shame leads to apathy, degradation of self, self-harm, or other numbing behaviors to avoid the pain.

Our responses to shame are the same as those evidenced by Adam and Eve in the garden.

Then the eyes of both of them were opened, and they realized they were naked; so they sewed fig leaves together and made coverings for themselves. Then the man and his wife heard the sound of the Lord God as he was walking in the garden in the cool of the day, and they hid from the Lord God among the trees of the garden. But the Lord God called to the man, "Where are you?" He answered, "I heard you in the garden, and I was afraid because I was naked; so I hid." And he said, "Who told you that you were naked? Have you eaten from the tree that I commanded you not to eat from?" The man said, "The woman you put here with me—she gave me some fruit from the tree, and I ate it." Then the Lord God said to the woman, "What is this you have done?" The woman said, "The serpent deceived me, and I ate."[4]

As they realized their vulnerability and inadequacy, their new state of disconnection and brokenness lead them to respond to the resulting shame in three different ways that seemed right to them.

First they withheld themselves from each other. They sewed fig leaves together and made coverings, so that neither could see the reality of who the other was. In effect, they were putting on a costume in order to limit exposure and earn the approval of the other.

When they heard the footsteps of God in the garden, an occurrence that likely would have been ordinary on any other day suddenly caused them fear. The relationship had changed. Where once there was trust, there was now doubt that God held their best interests at heart. *This led to their second response, which was to hide themselves from God among the trees of the garden.*

Think of the foolishness and desperation of trying to hide from God. Yet, every time we attempt to put our best foot forward when we talk to God, or try to find a place of isolation in order to commit a sin, we are following the same course. Withholding from God what is inside in order to cover shame.

It is interesting that Adam and Eve chose not to express sorrow. The first response of the false self is to try to make it better. This is an impulse I fight in myself when I stumble or struggle. Instead of opening up and communicating with God, my thought is to say that if I'm just good for the rest of the day, then I will be good enough to approach God.

Lastly, we see that the man and the woman hide from self. Instead of developing awareness of the root of what they did and taking ownership, each responds by seeking something external to blame.

Adam points to the woman. Simultaneously, he blamed the woman for his failure to live within God's established boundary, and blamed God for creating her. Rather than confessing the temptation of the Lie and the pride that it activated within him, Adam chose to discharge his pain and place it on the shoulders of the woman and God.

Not to be outdone, the woman did the same thing. As if she had no choice in the matter, Eve said that she ate because the serpent had deceived her. While it is true that there was deceit, she willingly abandoned the truth of who God is and of whose she was, and took the fruit in order to eat it.

Values and Desires

The false self needs a constant supply of worth and significance. It craves the affirmation, approval, security, and control that you were designed to live in through the image of God.

Shame becomes the ally of the false self.

Shame is an emptiness that must be constantly filled. Values are the filter between the source of identity and decisions, behaviors, and ways of relating to others. (See figure 4 below, The Tree of Lies.) As a response to a felt absence of worth, values and desires determine how you fight against, flee from, or freeze in shame. Hence the definition of what is right or wrong; what you say yes to, and the types of things that you decline. You begin to do what is right in your own eyes.

Truth becomes completely subjective.

Values and desires are consistent with the root of identity in order to provide what the false self needs for reinforcement. The fruit of the tree provides evidence of worth because the false sense of identity believes what it experiences.[5]

This is the reason that a pastor and follower of Christ, like me, who has knowledge of what is right or wrong in God's eyes, can make the decision that leaving his wife and pursuing another relationship is the right thing to do.

It is the reason that, despite the knowledge that Jesus came because of God's love for the world, James and John can ask if they should call down fire from heaven and destroy a village that had not welcomed them.[6]

It is the reason that a person attempting to numb their shame can eat more chocolate even though they know they need to lose weight.

It is the reason a businessman will say yes to staying late at the office even though he knows he hasn't spent quality time with his family.

It is the reason that all of us so often experience obstacles and frustrations in our discipleship.

What will bring a sense of significance to the self, or feeding the root, is deemed to be right. Situations that make you confront your shame or decrease your perceived value are judged wrong. Fruit that will detract from one's sense of self or other's perception of your worthiness will be hid.

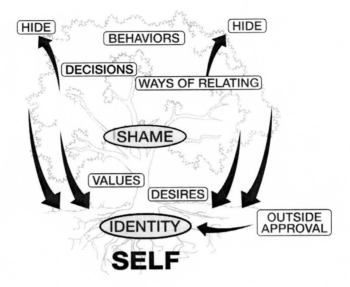

Figure 4 – The Tree of Lies

This is the contrast between being centered in God and centered in self.

Read through the book of Judges and you will see this pattern repeated over and over again.

- God makes promises to the Israelites and reminds them that they are His people.

- The Israelites are thankful for His intervention.

- After a time, they begin to do what is wicked in the eyes of God.

They sought fulfillment in other gods and wanted to be like other nations. Out of their disconnection with Who defined them, the Israelites begin to do what is right in their own eyes.[7] Rather than being centered in Him and reflecting His image to the world, they were centered in themselves.

Fast forward to the New Testament and we see Peter in the garden when the crowd came to arrest Jesus. At this point, Peter (and all the disciples for that matter) is still wrestling with who Christ is and what the benefit will be in following Him.

As soon as they try to arrest Jesus, Peter pulls out his sword and attempts to cut the head off the servant of the high priest, a decision that is consistent with his image of Jesus as political emancipator. Peter judged what was right or wrong based on what was going to bring value to him. Hence he chose to fight.

Values and desires also form the lens through which God is viewed. As we saw above in the Genesis 3 passage, the man and the woman blame God for the trouble of their situation. Even though God was not the source of the Lie, he became a source of blame for the outcomes.

Think of how often this is part of your own experience. You make decisions or enter into relationships without consulting God or taking inventory of where the significance is directed, but when this decision or relationship fails, you attack God for not caring or wonder where He is, or question His love for you. God will not be manipulated to bless the fruit that came out of your search for significance and wholeness apart from Him.

Functional Values

Because values protect identity, there is a consistency between the values that we have and where sense of self is rooted. When hiding from self, people have values that they state, but are in conflict with how they live. This comes from not having awareness of what identity is or where it is rooted. The values that you function by are your real values.

Decisions, behaviors, and ways of relating to others provide evidence of functional values. In the various roles that I have held with different churches, one of the things I have done is call people who were not in church for two or three weeks in a row. This was not an effort at shaming or condemning, but simply so they would know they had been missed and to see if anything was wrong. (And, I guess if I'm being honest with you and myself, I also wanted them to think how great it was that I had checked in on them.)

Most people saw this as an encouraging thing. Yet, sometimes, people would feel that they needed to justify their absence. In that event, they may start by saying *"church is the most important thing to me, but…"* That was the stated ideal, yet it was not evidenced in the way they were functioning. It cannot simultaneously be true that church was the most important thing if they were routinely making conflicting plans.

Dallas Willard wrote, *"Knowing the 'right answers' does not mean we believe them. To believe them means to act as though they're true."* The point of my reflection is not that you should be a church attendance legalist or that there aren't healthy and holy reasons to miss a church service. It is that these people were not being honest with themselves about the role of their values and desires. It was important for their identity to plan church conflicts and to not lose my approval.

The apostle Paul understood that his identity was in Christ, but he also understood the depths of the rooting in self that was within him. I think this is what he meant when he said that he knew what he wanted to do but did what he hated.[8] Rather than feeding self-condemnation, this is an opportunity to learn and observe and understand that there are parts of our identity that we have not yet given to Christ and investigate those parts. Healthy spirituality involves engaging the interior journey of developing awareness of who we are, instead of avoiding it.

The Trap of the False Self

These values and desires for self produce a cover-up. There is an image that all of us project to those around us as a way to gain approval and affirmation.

Adam and Eve covered with fig leaves. Now their spouse would only see what they wanted them to see. Rather than being naked, they could hide and withhold themselves from the other. There were now walls and distrust in their relationship.

Instead of the image of God, they were each projecting an image of their own creation. Sewing a covering out of fig leaves would take a lot of work. Just like the image that your false self manages.

In the Old Testament story of Joseph, we see a boy that had covered himself in the approval of his father. The outward expression of this approval was the multicolored coat that he was given. As Joseph flaunted his most favored status, his brothers' response was anger and jealousy and distrust. The covering matched Joseph's identity, and wearing the coat was the right thing to do in his eyes. His brothers' jealousy fed his sense of self.

As a person rooted in the approval of others, what did the cover-up look like? What was the image that I was portraying?

First, I was good at reading people and knowing what they wanted. So I was adept at being a relational chameleon. I would behave in a way that met a person's expectations.

Another behavior I employed was fishing for validation. Complimenting someone in the hopes of having something nice said in return. Or displaying a false humility to lead someone into building me up. These were learned strategies that built up my sense of affirmation.

In groups I was always the center of attention. This did two things: I would get the attention that I desired, and being what others wanted is a surprisingly good way to hide. While being laughed at or cheered for, people don't have the chance to know what is going on below the surface. For me, it was a win-win.

In personal conversations, I could hide through my ability to ask questions. It was very easy to deflect attention away from me—from having to talk about my problems and my struggles—by simply asking questions of another. People want to be known, and that was something that they liked about me.

Maybe my best example of how well I had covered up happened just a few weeks before I made a bunch of decisions that were harmful to me and my family and my church. I was at a small prayer group with a couple other pastors, and I was really wrestling with God. I knew what the right thing to do was, but what I wanted seemed to be filling my emptiness. So I asked the other guys there to please pray for me because I had some huge decisions that I was contemplating and I wanted to be clear on what I should do. I will never forget the response of one of the guys, who said *"Pray for you? You have it all together and do everything so well. You should be praying for us."* As I have grieved all the pain I later caused, I'll never forget how satisfied I was by his response.

My rootedness in peoples' opinion of me was sustained by my values and dictated what I allowed people to see. In order to maintain this image, vulnerability in my relationships became virtually impossible. I was using approval to feed the root of my identity (Figure 4), yet my values were producing comparison, dependence, insecurity, anger, and perfectionism that I was either ignoring or trying to work harder to stop.

This was a trap from which I could not break free, no matter how hard I tried.

In your effort to quench the unquenchable thirst of the identity rooted in self, you will get trapped by negative decisions, behaviors, or ways of relating that the false self either convinces you is a virtue (value) or to try harder to overcome (desire). Here are common snares I've encountered:

- Perfectionism. A corollary to the identity question "What do you do?" is "How well do you do it?" Value ascribed to performing without a flaw.

- Productivity. Another corollary to "What do you do?" This question is "How much do you do?" Judging self and others' value by how much is done.

- Consumerism. When significance is in the amount of possessions, there will be a pressure for more and more.

- Expectations. Relationships become anchored down when you need another to reinforce your value to them. When the other person (who is imperfect) does not measure up, you become disappointed.

- Busyness. This is the practice of avoidance of self, others, or God by incessant activity. This relieves the pressure of relational adequacy.

- Competition. Finding worth in being better than another spiritually, financially, relationally, physically, or in some other area.

- Comparison. Looking to see how you measure up in order to gauge significance. Comparison can be validating to the false self or a shame-builder, and thus reinforces insecurity, anxiety, and pride. How do your kids behave compared to the neighbor's? How many church activities do you do versus someone else?

- Gossip. Building yourself up by tearing others down.

- Anxiety. Grasping for control that is out of reach.

- Legalism. Adherence to a set of rules as a measure of wholeness. For example, the thinking that your obedience to traffic laws makes you a better person than someone who does not.

- Fusion. Also called enmeshment, this is worth determined by another's satisfaction with you. A person has no sense of identity apart from another.

- Isolation. Avoiding the risk of disappointment, either your own or of someone else's to your actions.

- Manipulation. Controlling others emotionally, financially, or some other way to get what you want.

- Scarcity. The feeling that there will never be enough, and so you conform to what will keep you from losing it. Money, friends, or followers are some examples.

- Fear. Not wanting negative consequences, punishment, judgment, or abandonment because of who you are.

- Niceness. Always putting on a good face, not confronting or being truthful in an effort to keep the peace.

- Sarcasm. A strategy to deflect vulnerability and keep another feeling worthless.

- Anger. When you are blocked from getting what you want or encounter an obstacle to satisfaction, the result is frustration or anger. You want what you cannot have.

To the false self, these traps seem right because they provide worth, motivation, or they protect significance. But in the end, each is a way that we use in an attempt to create wholeness apart from the Creator.

Failure and Struggle

In our culture, failure and struggle are viewed as a problem of not following Jesus "properly". Just as we expect in the business world, spiritual growth is supposed to be linear or exponentially positive and increasing.

Thus, we don't want people to know we are depressed or doubting. We hide our anger and disappointment rather than face it. There is an expectation that grief will be processed quickly. We tell people everything is great in our marriage even while we begin to resent or hate the person we are married to.

My coaching recently brought me in contact with a pastor of a fairly large church who wanted to know more about what I do. In our time together, I shared with him my story of burnout and I listened to his story of ministry and how he found himself in this particular church. As I was leaving, I asked him if there was any area that we could work on together. His response was simply that burnout was not a problem for him; he had a good support system and a right relationship with God. The image he wanted me to see and affirm was that of a put-together pastor who was doing everything right and having no problems.

About three months later, I checked in on him again and was told that he no longer worked at that church. Sadly, he could not manage the image any longer and had left the ministry. It made me so sad to think that he was so covered up that he couldn't respond to my story, which was similar to his. The worst part is that not only was he hiding from me and those around him, but he was also hiding from himself and God. He had refused to develop an awareness of what was going on under the surface and begin to take the interior journey.

Obstacles and struggle are assumed to be evidence of doing things wrong. While that tends to be the assumption, quite the opposite is true. Our weakness is an opportunity for Christ to be strong as we surrender our source of identity to Him.[9]

Failure and struggle provide a chance for us to develop awareness of what we are clinging to for wholeness as a first step to releasing our grip. This is a lifelong process that will often require two steps backward before making a fresh step forward.

Gain Perspective

- Describe an example from the news where blame was used to discharge pain or deflect responsibility.

- What other biblical story can you think of where someone did what was right in their own eyes? What was the perceived benefit?

- When do you commonly experience shame?

- Explain how "shame becomes the ally of the false self."

- What is a recent example of you using the blame strategy to avoid feeling worthless?

- What trap of the false self do you struggle with most?

- Explain how you have justified an action you know was wrong or would hurt someone else.

- In what areas of your life do your stated values conflict with your decisions and behaviors?

- Read Proverbs 14:12 and contemplate how it relates to the discussion of identity.

5 | Core Lies

What is the story you tell yourself?

On our way home, I was in the car with my young daughter when she complained about being hungry. In fact, hunger was fast becoming an urgent need in her world, and so she started crying. The errands that we had been running took longer than I had expected, but I had not brought any snacks. Is this how a good dad operates?

At this point, with tears streaming down her face, I started to get frustrated and told her not to cry since we would be home very soon. The more she cried, the more my frustration increased.

While from her perspective it may have seemed like I was upset with her, my daughter was not the source of my agitation. My battle was with the thought going on a loop in my head: "You are a bad dad." Instead of seeing the attempt to get the errands done without having a food plan as poor preparation or a mistake in judgment, it became a barometer of my worth as a person.

My daughter's reaction ignited one of the narratives that I tell myself: that I must earn people's approval. In essence, I am not likable apart from my performance.

It was the same core lie that caused me to respond to the problems in my marriage by constantly putting the impetus on myself to try harder. So if my wife wasn't happy, then it must be because I was not a good enough husband. If we went shopping and she did not buy an outfit that I picked out, it must be because my choice wasn't good enough. If my wife did not want to respond to me physically, then it was because I had not done enough around the house, or I had not performed well enough in some other capacity. Receiving love had strings attached that I controlled. (Many marriage books, particularly the popular ones, tap into this lie of control. If you do X for your spouse, then you will get Y as a response.)

I am not alone in being subject to a false narrative. One long-time client of mine struggled with the lie that everything being done right depended on her. If she did not do it, then either it would get done wrong or not get done at all. This lie fed her anger at her husband's perceived incompetence and forced her to oversee every detail that happened in the household.

Another example is a man who asked for my help planning his next career steps. His lie was that he was a disappointment, and so was frozen and unable to make a plan that reflected his strengths. Together we worked on helping him develop boldness to pursue the calling God had on his life.

Shame Builders

The false narratives or lies we carry at the core of our nature are questions we have that build shame. As a response, we attempt to prove these lies wrong by constructing a false sense of identity to answer them.

In my case, being a people pleaser was a response to the lie that I could not be loved nor accepted unless I earned it. I used my roles—husband, father, and pastor—as opportunities to seek worth and quiet the lies. When I failed at that, the story I would tell myself was that I was not trying hard enough. That no one will notice me unless I do something right. And then I would become sad and isolated.

Barbara (not her real name) sought coaching with me to learn how to function differently in her relationship, as well as overcome obstacles she was experiencing, in growing as a disciple of Christ. As she responded to my questions, it became clear that Barbara lived with the lie that nothing she did was good enough. In fact, this was a clear message impressed upon her by her mother and older sister from childhood.

When it came to men, Barbara would find familiarity in being treated as if she was not good enough. On her second marriage, she was responding to her lie by trying to be a 'biblical' wife, and then pleading with her husband to understand how good she was to him. His lack of satisfaction just reinforced her sense of shame.

In her relationship with Christ, she could not understand the concept of grace because she felt that she had not performed well enough to deserve it. If she could not please her husband and be a 'biblical' wife, how would Jesus be pleased with her as a follower?

The purpose in identifying your core lies is not in order to assess blame. Most lies develop simply because you have been raised by broken people that have created and replicated broken systems. The people who raised you and influenced you most likely did the best job that they could as they were battling with their own false narratives. At the same time, the problem is compounded by the fact that you are centered in self.

Becoming aware of your core lies allows you to be able to substitute and live in the truth of who you were created to be. Opening your heart to this reality will allow the Holy Spirit to shine light into the darkness.

With that said, while not one of blame, this process also provides the opportunity for you to work through offering forgiveness and releasing regret. If you are a survivor of intentional harm or abuse, that process would be best done with a counselor with experience in your area of trauma.

All of us are born into a world filled with two types of people: those who are trying to create their own sense of worth apart from God, and followers of Christ who are doing so imperfectly. Think of a baby's focus. Because it is helpless to meet its own needs, when a baby is hungry, it cries. Or when it needs to be changed, it cries. The only form of communication a baby has is to cry when it needs something. A baby does this because it has been conditioned to learn that when it emits a cry, comfort and security will follow from a caregiver.[1]

Yet, no parents, no guardian, and no caregiver, regardless of how good they are and how well they perform their job, can prevent a baby from ever crying. Needs cannot be met perfectly, and lies about self begin to be formed. As children grow up, develop the capacity to hold things to themselves, and have a life separate from those around them, the inability for needs to be met well constantly diminishes. This is related to the trust a child has for the caregiver to respond to the need. Additionally, children learn that worth is tied to performance. The ability to be obedient or live up to some external standard will provide a sense of acceptance. Hence, lies and the false self take shape.[2]

Core lies result from injuries to one's pride. Some come from injuries to the soul; wounds that are formed through abuse or neglect. Other hurts form from broken relational systems that cause negative circumstances or perceived injustices. Relating to others and interacting with their broken response forms false impressions of who you are.

Relational Systems

I was born to parents who loved me well. There has never been a time when I wondered if my well-being wasn't of the utmost concern to my father and mother. At the same time, they had their own brokenness and ways of dealing with the world that was inherited from their own parents.

The lies that I have believed about myself were not intentional, but rather the circumstance of life working in conjunction with the relational system and my own passion for self.

For most people this is also the case. Parents and caregivers did absolutely the best job that they could as they dealt with their own broken condition. Of course, there will be things that may merit forgiveness, or conversations, or learning to live in new ways. That is a part of the process of developing spiritual health.

It is within the family relational system that you have learned the skills and understanding—whether good or bad—of how to respond in a relationship.[3] Everyone transfers those skills to those they influence. There is a way that you are used to living. It feels familiar and comfortable to you, and because of your core lies, you will tend to replicate that relational system in your own relational world. This is what you would consider 'normal'.

Broken relational systems amplify shame. Whether it is a church relational system, family system, or some other group of relationships, there is a pressure to conform to some way of looking or behaving. This is why groups tend toward uniformity of some or all characteristics. Worth gets attributed to how one fits into the system. Within the family this may result from intentional strategy, as with a parent who is trying to get a child to succeed in sports or academics. Or, the shame may result from circumstance or memorable events.

For me, a memorable event occurred in first grade. I had a habit of telling on those who broke the rules. Despite being told that this was unacceptable in our classroom environment, I continued to act in this way.

One afternoon, after letting my teacher know that my neighbor had shared information with a friend, she called me up to the front of class. She proceeded to cut a long tail out of construction paper, wrote the words *"tattle tale"* on it, and pinned it to my backside. I then had to walk though the school with the tail on. You can imagine the rejection and failure this caused in first-grader me. This memory, that has been seared into my brain, was one part of many that contributed to the development of my false narrative.

An example of circumstance might be birth order. There is much research that links birth order with the tendency toward certain personality traits. (Keep in mind that because of the complexity of our design, there are no descriptions that are 100% accurate all the time.) Often, first children or only children are perfectionists because they have extended time with only adult examples.

Youngest children are often enabled as they are the babies, and therefore, have it somewhat easier because they don't have to tread the new ground of being the first child. Second children tend to excel differently than, or rebel against the example of the oldest as they blaze their own path. Middle children are often peacemakers and may see themselves as overlooked.[4]

All of this works to form the story that you tell yourself internally about how you are viewed. Everyone knows how they want to be perceived by others: competent, desirable, etc. But you also have an internal dialogue about how you think others are perceiving you. The narrative you repeat to yourself and what you truly believe tends to come out when something contradicts your values or interrupts your source of control, security, or acceptance.

Your lies have an impact on others. When Adam and Eve were created, they were made in God's image. Now outside the garden and experiencing the consequence of pursuing wholeness apart from God, they began to have children in their own likeness.[5] This is largely an unintentional process, but the lies get passed through the family system as children attempt to earn the approval of their parents. Now instead of reflecting the image of God, we are told that Adam was reflecting his own image. The broken image, the one that was filled with passion for self and a distrust of God, continued in the next generation.

In Maggie Scarf's example-filled book drawn from experience on this topic, she writes in *Intimate Worlds* that *"families often have recurrent, emotionally charged thematic concerns, whether these be 'inappropriate anger,' 'parental abandonment,' 'depression,' 'alcoholism,' 'inability to mourn effectively,' 'overclose attachment between a parent and a child,' 'difficulties in dealing with life's expectable separations and losses,' or any of a host of other problematic possibilities. These family issues are like emotional legacies, passed along from generation to generation, picked up here and there and worked upon anew by different individuals in different locations on the family tree."*[6] This idea is evident between biblical generations.

Abram and Sarai provide a good example. After renewing His commitment to build a people through Abram and Sarai, God renamed them Abraham and Sarah. Eventually, they do receive the child of the promise in Isaac. Out of jealousy Sarah asks, or rather demands, that Abraham send Ishmael and his mother away. This happens all in plain sight of Isaac. He knew he was the favored son. It is this way of father-son relating that becomes a generational pattern.

Later, Isaac, himself a father of two sons, displays the same favoritism. Esau, the first born of twins, is his favorite, and Jacob is sent away as an eventual consequence of this family structure.[7] Yet, the pattern does not end with this generation.

Jacob, who now has two wives and ten sons of his own, also has a favorite son. Joseph, who wore the robe of many colors as an expression of being the favorite. In a slight variation on the pattern, it is the favorite son Joseph that gets sent away by the brothers. But you can clearly see the generational pattern that had developed.

I became aware of this pattern in my own family during a conversation with my father. As I was embracing the development of my identity in Christ, I told my dad how much I loved him and wished that we talked in more depth to each other. His response was an eye opener to me as he said he wanted the same thing, but it was tough because he and his father never talked below the surface either. I had no idea that this was something that my father was carrying with him, and I'm glad we have worked to change this pattern.

What has happened to us as we grow in our family form the expectation of what will or should happen as we form our own, each generation having similarities that links it with the past.

False Narratives

As mentioned previously, the lies that you hold at the core of who you are determine how you perceive yourself and how you believe you are perceived by others. These false narratives are what you respond to as you form your identity and try to cover shame. Here are some of the lies about self that I have run across in clients, people I have worked with in churches, and within my own family system.

I am bad.

I am not good enough.

I am forgettable.

I am a disappointment.

I am unnoticed.

I am a failure.

I am worse than other people.

I am too much to handle.

I am unlovable.

I am a fraud.

I am stupid or wrong.

I am ugly or defective.

I am different.

I am unwanted.

It's my fault.

I can't be fixed.

I am good just the way I am and anyone who says different is wrong.

In each instance, shame forces a statement of being—"I am…" With identity based on "What do I do?", "What do I have?" and "What do people think of me?", something going wrong affects who you are rather than being a circumstance to respond to. So, instead of "I did something that disappointed someone," the narrative becomes "I am a disappointment."

When identity is based on a moving target, the result will be more feelings of worthlessness.

Hating Your Family

Jesus told the large crowd that was following Him that they must hate their father and mother, wife and children, and brothers and sisters before following Him.[8] Clearly and repeatedly we are taught to love one another, so what does this teaching mean?

Every one of us gains a sense of self from our relational system. We look to parents, siblings, a spouse, and our children for a sense of approval and validation. Hating means rejecting the lies of the system. You are to hate the relational system that worked alongside your own pride to work for your own wholeness.

You are not to long for the sense of wholeness and familiarity that the relational system provides. Doing things a new way, allowing Jesus to create a new relational system means rejecting the values of the old. In Christ you are adopted into a new relational system that is not based on performance or your own rightness.[9] Instead of believing and being subject to the core lies, Jesus offers a true response. In chapter 7 we deal with the subject of the truth of who you are.

But right now it is important that you identify what your core lies are, and also where they came from. That way you will be able to allow the truth and the light of Jesus to pour into those places and change the way you relate to yourself, and from that, the way that you relate to others.

The greatest commandment that you are given is to love God with your complete identity. Closely related to that is the command to love your neighbor as you love yourself. These two things are inseparable. If you don't love yourself, then you are choosing to not love something that God created for a purpose.

How Do You See God?

How you learned to relate to others will be projected onto your relationship with God. As I have said before, living as a people pleaser, I treated my relationship with Jesus in the same way. He was just another Person who wanted something from me so that I could earn approval. This created a relationship based on *MY* performance. I continually felt pressed to serve more, study the Bible more, pray more, and be seen as someone who did these things well. While I could tell people about the grace of God and help them find it in their own lives, grace was an experience that I was missing.

Another woman I coached provided another example of this. Because of the way she was raised and how her parents treated her and her siblings, she saw God as someone who loved some more than others. Her lie about God was that He plays favorites. Without realizing its origin, she was filled with anger when people experienced success in their relationship with God, and as she looked at her own life she was filled with resentment about why she could perform the way she did and still not be one of His favorites.

In addition to "I must earn God's approval" and "God plays favorites," here are other lies that form the basis of people's views about God:

God doesn't really love me.

God does not have my best interests at heart.

God is helpless to help me.

God is my buddy.

God is not good.

God needs to be placated.

God is out to get me.

God owes me.

God is the same as Santa Claus.

God is withholding.

God doesn't care about me, he just wants me to obey.

God is angry at me.

God is distant.

God is seeking to control me.

God cannot or will not forgive me for what I have done.

Identifying your misconceptions about God is the most important first step in becoming your true self. The pathway to enabling spiritual growth starts with who God is because it is a process He initiates and guides. "No matter how much we may want to change, until we see God differently we never will."[10]

It was only after I understood how I was viewing God and what I was projecting onto him, that I could begin to receive grace. Making that change required that I begin to change the narrative of my thinking by taking captive my thoughts and countering the lies with truth. I began actively partnering with the Holy Spirit to renew my mind in the image of my Creator.[11]

On my new journey to understanding the importance of having an identity rooted in Christ, I became aware that despite my mistake, despite me leaving my wife and hurting many in a church, I was still loved by God. This would not have happened if sitting in the pastoral counselor's office in Colorado we had not started with the question of who God was and did I think God understood my experience?

Both in harsh ways and in softened or weakened ways, this is how you create God in your own image. The image of God that you create comes with an expectation of how God will act, either doing things for you or being responsible for things done to you. Because of the characteristics of your earthly relationships, you have inherited a tendency to focus on one aspect of God's character above others and thus create a distortion of who God truly is. It may be choosing love over wrath, or vice versa. Or His justice and mercy may be seen to be out of balance.

Developing an awareness of how you think about God is necessary because it impacts your experience of Him. The person who has an image of God as a harsh Father will find excuses to not practice His presence. Similarly, if God is the One who distributes gifts like Santa Claus, then prayer will become a litany of demands and requests of a God who needs to do His duty.

Jesus makes this point in a pair of parables. While describing what the coming of the kingdom of heaven will be like, Jesus describes three servants who were given part of the wealth of their master while he was away. This is a picture of how the followers of Jesus use what has been given to them in His absence.

When the master returns, two of the servants respond by presenting back what they were 'entrusted' with plus what had been gained.[12] Their view of the master was one of trust and that what had been given was for a purpose. There is no fear in these servants and they are lovingly invited to share in the master's happiness.

The last servant, however, viewed the master as harsh. Because of that belief, he acted as if he were of no consequence to the master and used fear as an excuse for inaction. Rather than experiencing the master's happiness, the servant's fear led him to experience what his expectation had been.

In another story commonly referred to as The Parable of the Prodigal Son[13], Jesus contrasts the party that was thrown when the lost son returned home with the older son's dour reaction. The older son is angry that in all his years of obedience, the father had never given him anything to celebrate with, yet was now throwing a party for his irresponsible brother.

From the father's loving, gentle response to these accusations, it seems that the older son's mission to be seen as the 'good' and obedient son kept him from seeing the lavish generosity of his father. Rather than asking for and being given what the father would have willingly shared, this son experienced a deficit due to his faulty view.

Tilling the Soil

Your core lies about yourself and God stunt your spiritual growth. They compound feelings of being worthless and unlovable, and drive you toward self-protection. This is the soil of the false self. In order to enable growth you must confront these lies. It is not good enough to simply ignore them, for left alone, nothing will go away.

The lies will simply wait for an opportune time to come back to mind. Usually during a time of struggle or pain.

What is necessary is to rewrite the narrative that you have by renewing your mind in truth[14], breaking free of the pattern of the world that seeks to find answers to the lies and identity apart from God. Jesus is the source of life—your true self—because He is the image that relates the truth of who you are.

Learning to tell yourself a new story is an intentional process. One that is at times difficult and will feel awkward and uncomfortable at first. It takes practice, and you need to allow the Holy Spirit to testify to you about Jesus. As Counselor, Advocate, and Comforter, the Holy Spirit enables us to understand who we are in Christ when we are willing to open up.

You will become what you focus on, so fix your eyes on Christ and your decisions, behaviors, and ways of relating will follow.[15]

It is the truth that sets you free,[16] and taking hold of truth to shine into the darkness of the false self is the subject of the next section of this book.

Gain Perspective

- What lies about yourself and God from the list resonate with you? Can you think of any not on the list in this chapter?

- What circumstances or memorable events help form and/or validate those lies?

- Explain the difference between loving yourself and indulging yourself.

- Why are lies about how you think people perceive you easier to believe than the truth?

- Read the story of the prodigal son in Luke 15:11-32. What mischaracterizations of the father do you see displayed by the sons?

Part Three
The Truth

I praise you because I am fearfully and wonderfully made;
your works are wonderful,
I know that full well.

Psalm 139:14

6

God's Surprising Response to Brokenness

Who is the God you are following?

As He approaches where they are hiding, we get a great picture of the desire that God has for the man and the woman. He asked a simple question, *"Where are you?"*[1] Of course this question is rhetorical, for God knew exactly where they were and what they had done. *This question is an expression of His longing.* Asking for them to respond demonstrated that not only did the disconnection affect Adam and Eve, but it also impacted God as well.

The question "where are you?" resonates within our soul. When you are centered in yourself, perceiving nakedness as inadequacy and attempting to prove your significance, this question gets heard as a demand. Out of distrust for His goodness, God's question of longing becomes filtered and interpreted through your lies.

Where are you? I need something from you.

Where are you? I knew you would mess up.

Where are you? It is time to receive your punishment.

Where are you? I was busy doing something more important.

If the man and woman wanted to do their own thing, God could have left them to their own devices. But even though they had failed, God did not abandon them. Instead, He stood before them. Not as a towering giant, but as a concerned Shepherd.

When you begin to separate yourself from the lies to which you have been subject, you will see that God's surprising response to the fallen condition of humanity and to your brokenness is to step into it.

God enters in.

The Confrontation

When God approaches Adam and Eve, He does not fly off the handle nor tell them what their problem is. Instead, He asks them to confront their brokenness and become aware of where they had put their trust. The God who created the universe and sustained everything certainly knew what had happened. What we can learn about God from this event is that He engages rather than reacts.

God makes us confront our false self. Developing awareness is the difference between playing a part by putting on behaviors and changing our being by putting on Christ. This is His loving act of compassion for us, based on the knowledge that we were designed to be truly fulfilled, free, and at rest when our identity is secure in Him.

The battle is that we want God to bless the false self and make our pursuit of wholeness without Him more effective. He refuses to do this because He wants us to find our wholeness in Him.

In chapter one, I recounted sitting on the counselor's couch wondering if God understood my emptiness or was even aware of it. The more I talked that day, the more it became apparent what the basis of my problem was.

I did not understand God and His compassion.

I was raised in the Catholic tradition. For those not familiar, one of the doctrines of Catholicism involves confessing to a priest who then pronounces a penance—something that needs to be done to make your relationship right with the Father. Whether my young self rightly understood the doctrine or not, I am not sure, but the experience imprinted a false image of God in my mind. God's forgiveness needed to be earned.

Many years later, I was married and thinking about family, and I wanted to take ownership of my faith. But, the erroneous characteristics I had attributed to God were still stuck with me. While I was gaining knowledge, I had not addressed the truthfulness of the imprint I had; that false image was dictating my spiritual experience.

Part of the journey of identity is realizing that you cannot understand yourself until you understand who God is. God is knowable because He has allowed Himself to be. He wants us to know who He is.

Throughout the Bible we see a God who has taken the initiative to step into the experience of the brokenness of this world. God reveals himself and makes Himself known.

Mercy and Grace

God displayed his compassion for Adam and Eve by helping them to make a better covering out of the skins of animals. The first sacrifice took place at the hand of God; death of one living thing for the spiritual benefit of another was made so that the man and the woman could be covered. Mercy was shown by not leaving them to their own devices. Grace by giving them a helping hand in dealing with the new order of things.

Even after Abraham and Sarah had violated God's original covenant and tried to create descendants of their own, God returned and stepped into their distress. In fact, He reassured them that their descendant is going to be of both of their flesh.[2] At the same time, God reaffirms His own covenant with Abraham and Sarah. There was going to be a consequence, a mark in Abraham's flesh as a reminder of how he tried to create his own wholeness, but which would also provide a living reminder of God's mercy and grace.

Without a proper understanding of who God is, this reaffirming of the covenant may have felt punitive. If Abraham lived feeling like his performance was what mattered, then he would have felt pressured to be perfect.[3] Just as I felt in my own relationship with God. But with a right understanding, we can see that this was God lovingly demonstrating patience and continuing to make a way for Him and Abraham to be in relationship.

Even Peter, after he denied knowing Jesus three times, was a recipient of grace initiated by Christ. Instead of writing him off, an angel tells Mary at the empty tomb to tell "his disciples and Peter" what she saw.[4] Jesus chose to see Peter before the rest of the disciples.[5] In addition, Jesus restored Peter in front of the other disciples.[6]

This is why Jesus stepped into all of our experience by becoming flesh.[7] He came to seek and save the lost, and to reclaim what was His.

Reclaiming What Is His

Alienation from God is our primary problem.[8] Of course the most dramatic expression of God's longing to be with those He created is by the sending his Son, part of Himself, to live among us. Jesus' presence in this world is the ultimate parallel to the question that was asked in the garden, "Where are you?"

As Jesus drew more and more followers, creating trouble for the spiritual leaders of the day, the Pharisees attempted to trap Jesus and get him arrested. They publically asked Him if it was acceptable to pay the imperial tax to Caesar. To say no would have made him an enemy of Rome, solving the Pharisees' problem through Jesus' arrest. To say yes would have discredited Jesus and brought into question his allegiance to the God of Israel.

Here is how He answered:

"Show me the coin used for paying the tax." They brought him a denarius, and he asked them, "Whose image is this? And whose

inscription?" "Caesar's," they replied. Then he said to them, "So give back to Caesar what is Caesar's, and to God what is God's."

The discussion of the coin goes deeper than just the idea of making sure you pay taxes to Caesar. Nor is this a reminder to tithe. Jesus was appealing to the relationship between image and ownership.

Because the image of Caesar is on the coin, in this world it belongs to him. So if he wants the coin back, then give it back. But don't miss the weight of Jesus' next statement. *Since we were created in the image of God we belong to him.* Even though we are in this world, we belong to Him. Give back to God what is God's. Derive your identity from His image.

When Isaac was older, God asked Abraham to sacrifice the son he was given. This task was all about the source of Abraham's identity. If it was still in the results, Abraham would have conspired against God and withheld his son from Him. Instead, Abraham had learned trust, and with his identity secured, knew that God was responsible for the results. So, Abraham gathered together wood and began the trek to Moriah with Isaac.[10]

Redemption, the process of being made whole or worthy is accomplished through a reconciled relationship with God. It is not something we can initiate. God initiated with Abraham and He initiated with us. Through His sacrifice, Christ opened the path to reconciliation between us and God.[11] Because of His grace and mercy, God sees you in Christ without blemish.

Jesus had sent the disciples ahead to Galilee where He would be waiting for them. Peter had already seen the resurrected Jesus, both individually and as part of the group of disciples. Peter knew that he was forgiven, and he had heard the mission that Jesus gave to His followers. But once in Galilee, we hear Peter say "I'm going out to fish."[12]

Opinion varies on the implications of Peter going fishing. Some consider this another rejection of Jesus by Peter. Others see it as a simple pragmatic decision—Peter and the others were hungry. Considering the context of this chapter, I believe Peter's motivation was different. While he knew Jesus was risen, Peter thought that he had messed up too much to be used. So he returned to the thing that gave him a sense of worth.

This is our struggle too. We love Jesus, but struggle to give our full self to Him as we are pulled by the comfort, familiarity, and perceived benefit of the old self.

Without Jesus, Peter caught nothing. Your identity will be fruitless without the presence of Christ. When Jesus came on the scene and Peter did what He said, there was an abundance of fish.[13] Upon realizing that Jesus was on shore, Peter jumped from the boat and swam. *He still loves Jesus and must be near Him!*

After they ate, Jesus turned to Peter and asked him point blank, *"Simon, son of John, do you love me more than these?"*[14] What are "these" referred to in this question? It may be the other disciples, for Peter had once declared that even if everyone else fell away, he would not.[15]

While that has truth to it, I think Jesus was nodding toward the boats, nets, and fish. Jesus was saying, "Do you love me more than bringing in the catch? Do you love me more than your old way of life?" This was the opportunity of reconciliation for Peter. Where was he going to derive the meaning of his life?

Seeing God Clearly

Twelve men had taken up Jesus' call to follow. Yet, in the years leading up to the crucifixion, there was a lot of confusion about who Jesus was. The disciples' hope, derived from the culture of the nation, that Jesus was a military emancipator was blinding them to the truth.

In one of their conversations, Thomas asked Jesus to show them the Father and that would be enough to ease their anxiety and fear.[16] In response, Jesus asked how it is possible that they have not recognized the Father yet, for if they were truly seeing Jesus, then they were seeing the Father on display.[17]

The perfect God entered and lived in a broken world. The term for this is incarnation, and it is how God intended to restore the image that we live in. Jesus came as the image of the invisible God so that those without the spirit can see and understand the spiritual things of God.[18]

His purpose in coming was to give the disciples a right understanding of who God is, and allow them see themselves as His. That alone was going to define who they were and what their significance was. Jesus stepped into humanity's experience so you and I could see God. The person of Jesus stands in direct opposition to the lies and false images you have formed about who God is.

From Jesus, we learn about the patience of God. He taught his twelve disciples for three years, and while there were frustrating moments, Jesus did not demand any leave for poor performance. Instead, mistakes were treated as opportunities to learn more about themselves and God.

God is kind. Jesus treated the woman at the well gently. His compassion extended to the hungry that He fed and the sick that He healed. Throughout his time He developed friendships with those that followed Him and opened their homes to Him. No one, from children to women to outcasts, was overlooked by Jesus. In fact, those were the people Jesus identified with the most.

The nature of God is generosity. Jesus experienced the separation from God that we deserved. He gave his life, all that He had, so that reconciliation could be accomplished.

God is faithful. From His own mouth, Jesus said that He would be with His followers until the end.[19] When times got tough, Jesus did not run from the cup that was placed before Him. Even when everyone else left, Jesus faithfully found them.

The forgiveness of God is unending. One of the ways that Jesus got under the skin of the chief priest and Pharisees was His statement of forgiving sins. Offering forgiveness was of higher concern than obeying the Sabbath or healing physical ailments.

Of course this is not an exhaustive list, but it teaches you a new lens through which to read the gospel stories. After each verse or paragraph ask the following questions: "What does this teach me about who God is?" and "How does this differ from how I live in relationship with Him?" Keep a journal so you can watch your progress as you begin to uproot the lies.

In chapter twenty of the gospel that bears his name, John recorded his purpose for writing the events of Jesus life, death, and resurrection:

> *But these are written that you may believe that Jesus is the Messiah, the Son of God, and that by believing you may have life in his name.*[20]

What John wrote about was to help you and me overcome the lies that we have formed about who God is, some of the very same lies that the disciples and contemporaries of Jesus had to contend with. As you get a clearer picture of who Jesus is, then you can have full life in Christ.

Finding Life

In my case, the false impression of God kept me from understanding grace. I followed Christ as if grace was a one-time event that allowed me to enter the club. After that, I was living under my own effort and becoming spiritually malnourished.

In the previous chapter, I mentioned working with a client who believed God played favorites. This kept her from experiencing life in Christ because she felt like she needed to be in ministry to be of value to God. She believed that those who devoted their vocation to Him were the ones God favored. In an effort to be liked by God and affirmed by others, pursuing ministry began to form the root of her identity. Her decisions were being held captive by the lies.

During our time together we had to understand the origin of her impression of God and compare it with the truth. It is that truth that needed to form her new mindset, and together we developed several strategies to practice the truth. I'm not saying ministry wasn't in her future, but if she did not address this motive of the false self, then she was going to be filled with even more worthlessness and a growing sense of insecurity when her false self was not fulfilled in ministry. Seeing who God really was and how that differed from the way she was functioning was a foundational step.

Like these two examples, rather than fulfillment and wholeness in God, you may be trying to satisfy yourself. This is made worse by self-deceit that convinces you it is Jesus you are following.

Jesus talked about a group of people who He was going to stand before and say, *"I never knew you."* This group of people did not want their lives to be messed up and wanted to follow Christ on their own terms.[21] They avoided the intentional and sometimes painful process of developing awareness and surrendering to the truth of Jesus. The root of this group's identity was in self, but they had convinced themselves that they knew Christ. They were content to live creating their own sense of wholeness. Thus, by not living in the truth of who He is, they lived far from Jesus and He did not know them.

Calling On the Name of the Lord

So God has stepped into your experience, made Himself known, and then wants you to respond by drawing near to Him. Here's a promise: if you draw near to him, then he will draw near to you.[22] Choosing not to run away or not building walls of separation is part of the security of any intimate relationship. As you draw closer, you will be forced to confront your self-centeredness on a deeper and deeper level.

This is what theologians call the process of sanctification. God chipping away the rough edges as your true self is revealed. Like a sculpture, this is continually being refined, because you are God's workmanship—his work of art.[23] Being transformed requires remaining in the presence of the Artist.

Developing your identity in Christ necessitates living in the presence of God. He is the light that makes your root grow and develop and thrive. Being open to God is giving Him space in your life so that He can step in.

Elijah was a great prophet who lived before Jesus. His task was to confront the Israelites with the fact that they had run far from God. In the Old Testament book of First Kings, Elijah had an incredible confrontation with the prophets of the idol Baal, whom the Israelites were increasingly putting their trust in. After a miraculous display by God, an overwhelming victory, and the ending of a long drought, Elijah stood boldly.

But one of the leaders of Baal worship sent Elijah a threatening letter. With his success challenged, Elijah was scared and ran. As he was searching for answers and calm, Elijah was instructed to wait for the presence of God. There was a display of vicious wind, an earthquake, and raging fire. All of us want God to speak loudly, over the noise and busyness of our lives. Then we would not have to be so close to hear His voice. For Elijah, and for us, God's presence was found in a gentle whisper.[24] Being open to receive from God required Elijah to be still. Focusing not on himself nor his circumstance, but on drawing near.

Openness is the practice of being still. Not drowning out limiting beliefs and self-talk with more noise or activity. Having a stillness of mind where you are listening for what God says, and discipline of mind to respond to the lies with truth. Draw near to God and He will draw near to you.

There is a classic work called *Practicing the Presence of God* about a seventeenth century monk named Brother Lawrence. He was not considered smart enough or eloquent enough to be one of the higher monks, and so he was relegated to the kitchen to prepare meals. Rather than bitterness and frustration, Brother Lawrence used this as an opportunity to "practice the presence of God." This monk knew that God was everywhere, and so he used the work of making nightly soup as an opportunity to draw near God and understand Him better. Doing so was not easy nor something that always came naturally, but rather took intentional discipline. Using his work as a way to practice the presence of God was Brother Lawrence's mindset. The irony is that it is him we remember and not the monks who were considered more educated and wiser than he was.

Whatever it is you do, do it in the presence of God.[25] We have a tendency to compartmentalize our lives. Holy things get done at designated times. So, we schedule devotional time. Small group time. Church time. This leaves us with the mindset that the rest of the time is our time, or that God has less desire to be involved in other parts of our lives.

The compartmentalization of life allows time for the nurture of the false identity. If the drive to define self is through the question "What do you do?", there will be busyness and the inability to slow down and hear God. Perfectionism deafens you to the grace that God desire to lavish you with. Being driven by possessions creates a value out of hurry. Desiring the affirmation of others causes us to not be still and believe God's perception of ourselves. All of these attributes of the false self are the earthquakes, wind, and fires of life that cause you to miss the compassionate and nurturing voice of God.

Being open to God means developing the ability to be present with him in everything you do. Opening yourself to Him continuously. Developing your relationship in prayer. Praying is not primarily a list of requests. Or solely a list of what you have done wrong. Approaching prayer like that alone is to swoop in like a tornado, get what you want, and leave. That is not developing presence.

Prayer is being present with God. Relationships are built by creating space in order to listen. This may be tough because your mind wants to bring things to the surface when you are quiet. How often do you listen for response? This is much harder, because control is no longer yours.

Everything that happens in life is an opportunity to draw near to God and have Him be a part of you. God *wants* to be invited to be a part of it. How do you practice the presence of God while driving the kids to school? How do you hear the small whisper of God when you are at the office? How is God involved when the opportunity for a conversation with someone interrupts your task list?

If slowing down and creating space to be present with God creates anxiety within you, or if your first impulse is to push back with all the reasons that being still is impossible, then you have the first place to focus awareness on your false sense of self. There is competition in your life for the attention of the One who wants a relationship with you.

A Spiritual Mindset

Being a disciple of Christ "is not a question of our own doing, it is a matter of making room for God so that He can live in us."[26] Loving God, or worship, is often seen as the idea of doing something for God. If love consists of the idea that your actions must bring God glory, it makes it about you and what you do for God. What you do for God is the object being magnified.

To worship something is to draw your sense of self from it. Worshipping God is about being certain about who you are by developing your identity. From that state of being rooted in the image of God, actions and relationships that make the name of God great will pour forth.

Instead of trying to prove how much you love God, learn to rest in how much God loves you.[27] As you surrender your brokenness and lies to truth, Christ is able to increase. A priority on doing leads to conformity, being in His presence leads to transformation. This is a change of mindset that it is not about what you have done for God, but rather what God has done for you.

Before renewing His covenant with Abram and Sarai, God changed their names. Now every time they addressed each other, it would be a reminder of what God had done for them. In fact, these new names were also a reminder of the truth about who they were in the Lord: Abraham meaning "father" and Sarah meaning "princess."

Hundreds of years later, when God fulfilled his promise to Abraham's descendants and parted the Jordan river so that they could enter the promised land on dry ground, He made a request. A representative of each tribe was to place a stone on a pile by the bank of the river. This simple pile of rocks was to serve as a reminder to the Israelites and to future generations of what their Savior had done.

The Psalms read like a journal of God's activity and the author's emotions. In response to feeling forgotten as if the Lord was wavering on fulfilling His promises—in other words, a crisis of faith—the author of Psalm 77 wrote that he would intentionally "remember the deeds," "consider all [His] works," and "meditate on" what God had done. From this mindset his strength would be renewed.

In addition to knowing the truth of who God is, a part of renewing your mind and changing the false narrative is to keep a remembrance of what God has done for you queued up or made easily accessible. And then practicing this new story.

As I began the long journey of earning back the trust of my wife and some friends, one of the core truths that I clung to and repeated is this: Jesus is the Author and Perfector of my faith. This was not an easy process because there was a lot of rejection and some people refused to forgive me. In that environment, it would have been very easy to revert back to doing whatever it took to earn approval. Even my failure would not be a reason for Him to abandon the project of sculpting me into my true self.

For my client who believed that nothing she did was good enough, the new narrative involved constantly remembering the grace of God. God would not love her more if she performed well nor love her less if she wasn't perfect. His love for her was not based on her performance, but on who God was.

God wants to perfect your faith. This process necessitates you releasing the false images of who he is and renewing your mind in the image of your Creator.

God delights in you. This is why Jesus experienced the silence that you deserved as He hung on the cross. This is Grace.

God stepped into the brokenness of this world and experienced its rejection so that you would come to know Him. In Christ, God gave you everything He has to give.

Gain Perspective

- Read Luke 8:40-56. What does this passage teach you about God?

- How do you make room to practice the presence of God?

■ What does your prayer life tell you about who you think God is?

■ How do you keep a remembrance of God's work in your life?

■ Find a quiet place where you will not be interrupted by cell phone, people, computer, or any other distractions. Take 15 minutes to be perfectly still and quiet. When thoughts attempt to get in the way, turn from them. Make space for God. After finishing, reflect on:

» What was difficult about this exercise?

» What thought kept trying to encroach on your solitude?

» What does that teach you about yourself?

7

The Desert Life

Who does God say you are?

God's people had spent four hundred years imprisoned in Egypt. When they remembered whose they were they began to cry out. God heard them and gave them a deliverer. Moses himself was filled with doubt, questioning how he could lead people and confront Pharaoh when he struggled to speak. Moses' view was that his weakness made him unusable. His lack of trust frustrated the God who had called him.

Stepping into their identity as God's people was not an easy journey. They were freed from the old order of things, and because of their faith they walked through the parted waters of the Red Sea. This was a baptism of sorts; a reminder of the power of God to take what was once dead and raise it to new life. The nation of Israel was born through those waters. Yet, during their miraculous journey the Israelites still struggled with trust. Ignoring that they had been slaves, they looked back and longed for the meat that was in their pots, and they grumbled against their leader and against the God who had sent him.

Walking into the Promised Land was to be the fruit of their restored identity. The Israelites needed to thirst for God more than they thirsted for the comfort of what was previously known. They needed to want God more than just wanting the benefits of knowing God.

Even after crossing the Red Sea and entering the land, they still did not fully embrace their identity as God's chosen nation. Because of this, God led them in the desert for 40 years. God's top priority was not their destination, but rather, transformation of their desire. They had to release their grip on what was comfortable and familiar so that they could step into the new life that God had for them.

The false self gets torn away piece by painful piece. This is how God uses the desert wilderness.

The Purpose of the Desert

A desert is a place of dryness and barrenness. Because of the sparse resources in the desert, it is difficult to find what you need. Given that it is so dry, the primary concern becomes quenching thirst.

Spiritually, the same thing is true. All of us are consumed with satisfying our thirst. We were designed to live in relationship with God, and our souls long for intimacy with Him. Yet, as we have already seen, our false self pursues wholeness apart from God. We may be living in a desert of our own creation.

Disconnected from God, we don't know who we are so we seek to define ourselves by experiences, successes, roles, relationships and things that this world tantalizes us with. Those are the mirages of the desert that leave us unsatisfied and wanting more. Like drinking salt water. The only result is that they do nothing but pull us further and further away from God and the true self He created.

God, out of His love, will give us over to the desert of our desires with the hope that we will want Him. Just like He'd done with the Israelites, who, because of their false desires for the security of their old life, were left to wander in the desert.[1] The desert draws out either a thirst for God, or a thirst for more self.

It is common to hear people talk about finding themselves. That is a surprisingly apt description of what humanity is going through in this desert wilderness. There are only two choices: look to the one true God to quench the thirst of your dry root, or try to satisfy the thirst yourself.

My desert was the void of affirmation, feeling noticed, and of being accepted. I was living my life pursuing ways I could provide those things for myself. When affirmation and affection were not available to me in my marriage or my role in the church, I began to struggle to know who I was or why I mattered. As my root sought to quench my thirst through more of my own effort, I became oblivious to the truth of who God said that I am.

As you follow your deliverer Jesus and are baptized into his body, you too are often led into a desert as you are made aware of the things that you cling to for pieces of wholeness. God uses the desert as a tool to release your grip on the old ways of the false self and refine your thirst for Him. Has your response been to look back and grasp harder?

By taking things away, you are able to see more clearly and your faith can increase. Abraham was asked to leave his father's house and go into the wilderness. Joseph was brought into Egypt and had to confront life apart from his father's favoritism. Before becoming king, David lived and fought in the wilderness to refine his desire for God over having power.

As each was asked to follow Jesus, the disciples left family, jobs, and community. Expressing the lack they felt, Peter (who else, right?) reminded Jesus that they left everything to follow Him.[2] In order to allow them to see Him more clearly, Jesus had separated them from everything they had formerly drawn life from.

Jesus in the Desert

The gospel of Luke records that Jesus was led into the desert as well. The timing of his walk into the desert is not insignificant, for Jesus had just been baptized and received affirmation of His identity from the Father. In His words to Jesus, the Father declared that Jesus was His Son, and also that He was pleased with who the Son was.[3]

In the desert, weakened in body through hunger and thirst, Jesus experienced the temptation of his identity.[4] When the enemy first approached Jesus, his first words were a confrontation of who Jesus is. *"If you are the son of God..."* It is a demand for proof and a statement meant to erode trust. It is precisely the same tactic that the serpent used in the garden. It is the same struggle that we endure through the lies that form the narrative of our minds. *If you are...*

This is the battle of identity.

In the epic scene, Satan spoke to each of the questions of identity. It started with the devil asking Jesus to turn a rock into bread. In essence, he was asking Jesus to define who He is by what He does. It was an invitation to create His own sense of control apart from the Father.

The enemy next took Jesus to a high mountain top to survey the cities and landscape. Looking at Jesus, the devil offered to give his borrowed authority to Him if He will just find His worth apart from the Father. The devil asked for Jesus' worship. If Jesus craved popularity, if He sought to create a positive answer to "What do people think of me?" then this would have been enticing. This was an invitation to create His own sense of affirmation.

Finally, Jesus was brought to the top of the temple and asked to throw Himself to the ground. The enemy said, "If you are the Son of God, then you have the protection of the Father. Put God's promises to the test." Jesus was invited to create His own sense of security.

In each instance, rather than remain silent or trying to ignore the lies, Jesus answered the false statements with truth. His mindset was firmly on the Father and finding the source of who He is—His identity—in the truth of who God has said He is.

Notice that when the Father expressed His approval of the Son, Jesus had not yet begun His ministry. This favor was not based on what Jesus had done or would do, it was based on who He was. Jesus was God's Son.

Like Jesus, you are not defined by what you do. Your identity is likewise not based on what you have. Your definition of self is independent of what people think about you (or what you think people think about you). Who you are is based solely on what God says. It is who God says you are that is important. Jesus is the truth about you.[5]

The thirst your soul has, the thirst that God is trying to refine in the desert, is the thirst for the waters of life. The truth about who you are.

Finding Life in the Desert

Within the fourth chapter of John's gospel, Jesus initiated a life-changing conversation with a woman drawing water from a well in the Samaritan town of Sychar. In this conversation, Jesus attempted to highlight for the woman what her true thirst was.

The woman was used to practicing avoidance, as evidenced by her action of doing the hard labor of getting water at noon by her-self. Not only did she live in the desert, she existed in a spiritual and relational desert as well.

This woman who was so used to putting up walls attempted the same tactics with Jesus. She pointed out that Jews and Samaritans, particularly Samaritan women, do not talk. All she wanted was to get her work done without bother.

Jesus responded to the woman's rebuff by telling her that if she knew to whom she was speaking she would have asked for living water. He was offering her the refreshing, life-giving water of truth. The answers to her questions of identity, why she had significance, and what her purpose was in the world were in Him. It was the offer of hope.

In her passion for self, this woman, like all of us, asked Jesus to change her circumstance. Asking for the water so she won't have to come to the well was an indication of her focus. Like her, we want the path of least resistance and ask for the false self to be blessed. But, the goal of Jesus was to highlight her true thirst, so He asked her to go get her husband.

Now it is evident that this was where her root was planted. She'd had five husbands and was presently living with a new man.

Rather than knowing how God saw her, she had been content to see herself as someone who needed companionship to be complete. This led her to be used and discarded until she was living with such shame that she could not draw water when the rest of the town did. That day, the woman's identity was restored through the truth Jesus offered, and she stood *without shame* before the town and led them to Jesus as well.[6]

Psalm one uses the imagery of a tree rooted next to a stream of water. Such a tree will not wither or burn out. With roots entrenched near the source of life, the tree will bear appropriate fruit at the appropriate time. Your fruit is the decisions, the behaviors, and the way that you relate to others and to God. According to Psalm one, with identity rooted in the image of God, you will not seek the affirmation from the wicked, nor find significance in the same way as those who sin, and the truth of God will bring you delight.[7]

This same Psalm goes on to talk about the wicked. All of us have an image of what a wicked person looks like, but none of us would dare consider ourselves wicked. It is a very harsh word. Being wicked means denying the goodness of God. Wickedness is pursuing wholeness apart from the Creator. Left to our own devices, all of us are prideful and wicked.

I had made a choice to not live in truth, to cover my own shame, and to pursue wholeness apart from the One who loved me. Out of fear of rejection, I could not let anyone know me. I was living an act, and it was the act people loved, which fed my sense of isolation and rejection. The result was burnout. My leaves had withered.

As I committed to the path of developing awareness of my identity and seeing myself as God sees me, I made the intentional decision to keep in the front of my mind the favor and grace that Jesus had extended to me. It was immersing myself in the living waters. The result was freedom and confidence, and the ability to delight in who God has made me to be.

In *Shaped by the Word*, Mulholland writes that God opens toward us, and we offer ourselves in return. However, this is something that takes place at a relational level, not the functional; at the *being* level, not *doing*; and the nature of being in relationship is formational, not informational.[8] Being immersed in truth is not about doing more, it is letting that truth become the basis for your identity. Hiding the word in your heart is not an injunction to see how much of the Bible you can memorize; rather, it is internalizing the truths of God's word and making it part of your being. Cooperating with the Holy Spirit to change your mind-set.

Finding your true self will not come as long as that is what you are looking for; instead, your new self comes when you are drawing near to God.

Drinking the Living Waters

Just like Jesus' temptation, the enemy is constantly attacking your identity.

- "If you were a good Christian, then you wouldn't be lonely or depressed."

- "If you were really a follower of Christ, then you could ignore you physical desires."

- "If you are really a child of God, then bad things wouldn't happen to you."

- "If you are really saved, then you wouldn't struggle with sin."

- "If you are loved by God, then _____." (fill in what first came to mind).

These conditional statements are the same tactic the serpent used in the garden to get Adam and Eve to doubt God.

Learning to live in who Christ says you are is a process of renewing your mind. You have to unlearn who the world has said you are, why it says you are valuable, and what are the areas it says give you identity.

Once you stop attempting to conform to culture's standards, then you can be transformed by truth.[9] Transformation is not storing up more information, it is being influenced by the truth you do know. Faith is the ability to be confident of these truths even when circumstance might try to convince you otherwise.[10]

As we saw in chapter 5, shame builds false statements of identity. Clothed in Christ, God sees you first and foremost as righteous and clean. Your existence is a pleasing aroma to Him.[11]

Christ has become your covering. Underneath the covering, every one of us is working out our salvation. We are saints who struggle with sin.[12] This must form your mindset. Not a mindset that gives you permission to do whatever you want, but one that works in conjunction with grace as we understand God and His love for you more and more. From the grace that you live in continually in Christ, you have a true source of self-compassion.

You are not defined by failure; you are defined by truth.

In his letter to the Roman church, Paul says to have your mind set on the Spirit.[13] Paul appeals to mindset in his letter to the Philippian church[14] and to the Colossians.[15] The difficulty in changing focus is noted in his words to the Corinthian church where he instructed them to take captive their thoughts. Your old thoughts have to be treated as your prisoners and forced to be obedient to the truth of Christ.

There must be a truth that you preach to yourself. Particularly as your identity is tempted and you want to go back to the decisions, behaviors, and ways of relating that are comfortable and have a quick pay off.

Because one of my lies is that I am unnoticed, I take encouragement that despite the relative insignificance of the sparrow, God takes notice every time one falls to the ground.[16] He knows me so well and has seen me so completely that even the hairs on my head are numbered by Him.[17] This is a truth that I absorb.

Every morning when I wake up, before my head leaves the pillow I tell myself that God notices me and cares about what is going to happen to me throughout my day. I also keep at the forefront of my mind that I do not have to earn His approval because I already have it in Christ. Hence, God's love is not dependent upon my performance or earning His attention. It may sound silly, but this habit reminds me to engage the world from the truth who Christ says I am.

At the end of each day I have made it my habit to do a daily examen. An examen is a set aside period of time where I reflect on my day and look for times when I sensed God's presence, as well as times where I was responding to the lies. My practice then is to write about it in a journal as a way to learn and process how I should do things differently next time.

One of my coaching clients felt that in her marriage she needed to be perfect in order for things to get better. After a few weeks she began to develop the habit of remembering that God does not expect her to be perfect, so it is unfair for others to place that burden upon her. In particular, she was drawn to how Jesus responded to Peter after his denial. Also, she was drawn to the fact that Jesus wept with the pain of others. Grace, she learned and began to experience, was available to her even when she didn't live up to expectations. When she realized she didn't cause her husband's choices and behaviors, there was an intentional, awkward shift in her thinking. Ultimately, she felt freedom in realizing that her actions were not as powerful as she had perceived.

Who God Says You Are

The pages of the New Testament have a lot to say about who you are in Christ. Because you are clothed in Christ and marked by the Spirit, your standing before God is righteous.[18] That is the way God sees you, not because of the things you have done, but because you are covered in the Son.

God came to get you. This was not something that He had to do, it was His choice because He is love. Christ's rescue of those separated from God shows that you are worth loving.

No longer strangers or enemies of God, you have been adopted by Him. You are in the family with the full rights and benefits of an heir. God has changed the old family system that you inherited. You are no longer defined by your family of origin.

You have every spiritual blessing in Christ. God the Father has given you every good and perfect spiritual gift. On your behalf, Christ was sacrificed so that you could be complete.[19] The wholeness that your soul has longed for and you have struggled so hard to create yourself is now yours. You are no longer defined by what you do, what you have, or how others perceive you. Instead, you have been invited into Christ's rest.

Guilt or fear does not follow you any longer because you have been forgiven. Your sins are as far from you as the east is from the west.[20] God has forgotten them because Christ now sits at the Father's right hand and speaks as one who understands your situation, because He, too, lived in this world.[21]

You have been made clean by Christ.[22] Spotless and without the blemish of sin, there is now no condemnation for you in Christ. Jesus has called you His friend; He has chosen to be your friend. Thus, you are accepted. Acceptance does not mean that God wants you to stay the way you are, for He loves you too much to allow you to settle. You are being lovingly shaped and formed in the image of His Son. This is the process in your life of which Jesus is the Author and Perfector.[23]

These are just some of the truths about who you are in Christ and should form the basis of your thinking about yourself. While not an exhaustive list, these statements about your true self can begin to speak to your lies. For more biblical statements regarding who God says you are, see Appendix B.

For a video resource and worksheet to help you create your unique Identity Statement in Christ, go to http://treeoflies.com/identity.

Through the Desert

You have been created uniquely. With talents and experiences that set you apart, this is the self that you are supposed to love. Loving yourself means that you know who God created you to be, and you are thankful.

You are to walk your own path, not walk or long for the path of somebody else. Wide is the path that tries to be like everybody else and to fit in. Narrow is the path that was created for you, for only you can walk it.

Shortly after Jesus restored Peter, He told him what he was in for. Peter was going to be led to a death he would not want on account of his response to Jesus' invitation to follow. Upon hearing this, Peter looked around and saw another disciple, and then asked Jesus, *"Lord, what about him?"*[24]

Peter's first inclination when he found out about the path he was to walk was to compare himself to someone else. The old nature runs very deep.

Comparing your spiritual journey, background, gifts, or calling to another will only lead to feelings of inadequacy or pride. There will be unnatural pressure to conform—inauthentic discipleship. This is why Jesus responds to Peter in the above story by not answering his question. Rather, He tells Peter that it is no concern of his what is in store for the other disciple.

Because of your unique design, the way you approach God and the way that you experience Him are going to be different from that of others.

This has been a very powerful realization in my own life. For instance, almost every time I had been taught about prayer it came from the vantage point of the necessity of praying first thing in the morning, on your knees, and in a dark, quiet room. A certain format was proposed for prayer to be acceptable. Certainly there is value in having this as part of a repertoire or routine. But, this mode never worked for me. I would fall asleep. Never was my design considered as part of the equation.

It wasn't until I read *Invitation to a Journey* by M. Robert Mulholland that I began to understand that there was not a one-size-fit all recipe for spirituality. The way I have been created is not something to reject or ignore, but to relish. Movement is natural for an extrovert, so I felt emboldened to walk while I prayed. Sometimes while on a hike enjoying nature, other times just on the sidewalk in my neighborhood. The motion kept me focused on God. Often I have a verse that I contemplate and savor. During my walking time, I can hear the small whisper of God. Of course there are times when I'm alone and it's dark and it's quiet, but that is not my normal way to pray.

Similarly, because of my need for approval whenever I would speak, I would try to conform myself to the style of others. I'd compare myself with those who were funnier or had a different style, and feel dejected. I would avoid my natural style, which is more oriented on teaching. I'm a teacher and synthesizer—good at drawing ideas together and communicating complicated ideas in understandable terms. It took me a long time to be joyful speaking the way I was made to speak. Yet, stepping into the way I was designed made my speaking more effective and impactful.

This has been part of my path of learning to love myself well.

There are many tools that can help to describe facets of the way God designed you. The Myers-Briggs, which Mulholland appeals to in the book mentioned above, is just one facet. There is the DISC test, Strengthfinders, the enneagram, temperament tests…and the list goes on and on. I am not endorsing one test over another, but I am encouraging you to develop awareness of how you have been designed. Whatever descriptor you choose, the key is to incorporate the results into your spiritual life.

On the cross, Jesus experienced the isolation from God and thirst for communion with the Father so that you could draw near to Him. Understanding your construction allows you to step toward Him in the way He intended.

Gain Perspective

- Read Matthew 9:35-38. What does this tell you about who God says you are?

- What do you think about when you hear the expression "I need to find myself?"

- How does the enemy tempt you to finish this sentence: *"If you really are a disciple of Jesus, then…?"*

- As you experience the desert of this world, where is your frustration originating? What is causing you anxiety? Where is your insecurity rooted? When do you experience anger? Make a list. These are symptoms of attempts to misplace identity and places to focus truth of gospel.

- In what areas do you compare yourself to others?

- What truth about who God says you are do you find hard to accept?

- How can you keep truth at the forefront of your mind?

8 | Planting a New Root

What does it mean to deny yourself?

If you were to ask me which biblical character I most identify with, my response would have to be the disciple Peter. This feeling has nothing to do with his being given the keys of the kingdom or his place of leadership in the early church. It is not an identification with or hope for status or success. Rather, Peter is my favorite due to the fact that no one failed as boldly, as repeatedly, and as visibly as he did. Through it all, Jesus kept working with and offering grace to this disciple.

There is a particular encounter between Peter and Jesus to which I am drawn. Jesus had just asked his disciples what the word among the crowd was concerning who He was. In reply, they gave a variety of answers: "Elijah", "John the Baptist", and "one of the prophets" among them. Suddenly, Jesus asked the disciples point-blank who they thought He was. It was Peter who characteristically jumped in with both feet and replied, "You are the Messiah, the Son of the living God."[1]

Jesus affirmed Peter's statement and went on to provide more details of what was waiting for them as they approached Jerusalem. There was going to be an arrest and Jesus was going to be put to death. Now Peter, only moments removed from declaring Jesus as the Messiah, pulled Jesus aside and told Him how wrong He was. "Don't you remember the Messiah thing I just said, you must be making a mistake." Knocked from his high horse, Jesus told Peter to stand behind Him, for avoiding death is the idea of the enemy.

Submitting His life to the leaders was not the picture of Messiah that Peter had in mind. In his response to Jesus, Peter was focused on himself and the benefits Jesus brought to his life. In just a matter of a few moments, we see Peter responding from his connection with God, and then from his old nature. When he told Jesus that this was not going to happen, Peter was responding from that part of him that wanted to sit at Jesus' right hand and enjoy the benefits of power. Being ready to usher in a new era of government for the nation Israel, Peter wanted to restore the success and glory of Israel from the days of David and Solomon.

After Jesus told Peter that his attitude was misaligned, He went on to describe discipleship.

Denying Your Self

What does it mean to be a disciple of Jesus? The first thing that Jesus says is that whoever wants to be his disciple must deny themselves.[2]

The idea of denying oneself seems to be so often misunderstood in both its teaching and in its reception. For some, denial of self carries with it the idea that you must abstain from certain behaviors. Denying self gets reduced to not going to parties, wearing particular clothes, eating certain foods, or doing anything that is not a sanctioned church event. In this case, discipleship is equated with a list of dos and don'ts.

Other times, the command to deny oneself gets applied to desires. For instance, instead of discerning that sexual desire was given a proper context to be enjoyed, sex is deemed dirty or a desire that should be repressed. The problem is that such a view leads to shame in areas in which there ought to be none. God made sex to be enjoyed. It is not the desire that is wrong, but rather, how that desire is pursued relative to identity.

Following a prescribed set of rules or behaviors is a way of adopting a religious life. Religion is a beautiful way to manage symptoms of a bad root. It gives you control while maintaining the appearance of following God. You receive validation from others that you are doing everything right, but inside you are far from God.[3] Ultimately, religion is just a new look for the false self. When you make your own way, God recedes into the background.

Still, others treat denying self as the need to put themselves down. Allowing themselves to be tread upon by others, or never saying or believing anything good about who they are. Self-flagellation is a product of freezing in shame, not a denial of oneself.

None of those responses gets to the core truth of what Jesus is talking about. When Jesus said, "You do not have in mind the concerns of God, but merely human concerns," Jesus was instructing Peter that denying oneself means denying the old self and its pursuit of wholeness apart from God. It is uprooting from self as the source of significance.

The command to deny oneself is a reminder of identity.

Self-denial means releasing your grip on control. Worry will not change the outcome; it is a product of trying to be in control. It is realizing that you can't make people behave a certain way in response to you. Nor can you manipulate God into giving you what you want.

You are to deny self as a standard of rightness. Judging other people's behaviors based on your own and living in contempt must be rejected. Self-righteousness is not wise and is the product of an identity rooted in self.[4] Righteousness belongs to God alone.

Denial of self means abandoning the things of this world as a source of security. Not looking to money, possessions, relationships, or followers to reduce anxiety. Security comes from knowing that you will never be let go of by Jesus[5] nor will He ever leave you or turn His back on you.[6]

The irony of trying to decrease anxiety with money, possessions, relationship, followers, or something else is that more will never be enough. Constant maintenance and protection of what you have is required. There will be a new model of phone or TV within a month. Markets crash and money disappears. Followers need to be kept happy. All of this augments rather than diminishes anxiety.

In order to deny yourself, you must embrace your weakness. Live every moment in the awareness that you are not God. Weakness is admitting your need for His grace.

Jesus told a curious story to illustrate what it means to deny self.[7] Two men are in the temple to pray; one is a spiritual leader and the other is a tax collector. At once, the people listening to this story would have made an immediate gut judgment about who is worthy to be praying in the temple. Tax collectors were cheaters and traitors, among the least respected in Jewish culture. But when Jesus described the prayer of each, the men's views of God and themselves were not what the audience would expect.

The leader spoke in terms of what he had done, and thanked God that he was not bad like the others, such as the tax collector in particular. He had built himself up into the standard of rightness, and his wholeness was clearly rooted in his own behavior. On the other hand, the tax collector simply asked for mercy, knowing that he was a sinner. This was a prayer of trust in the goodness and forgiveness of God. The tax collector was looking up toward God for identity rather than into himself.

We do this with more than religious rules. When we measure ourselves by some standard of identity, we perceive people through the same lens. Thus, thoughts like "my political party is right and you are a fool for voting for another" exist. When adopting a new fitness or eating regimen, people begin to look down on those who are "not healthy."

Humility is the ability to deny self, knowing that IT is not about you, and that Jesus came to show you that IT is about God. This is not denial of your worth. It is decreasing so that He might increase; in other words, creating space in your life so that God can fill it.

When you admit your weakness, developing awareness of what the temptations of your identity are, then Jesus gets the opportunity to be your strength.[8]

In the previous chapter, I mentioned that in following Christ each of us is to follow our own path, that it's not about conforming to a certain set of behaviors. But Paul says to *"Follow my example, as I follow the example of Christ."*[9] Aren't we then to act like Paul? What is the example of Christ?

Jesus is God in the flesh. Leaving heaven, Jesus walked among the people of earth for more than thirty years. He submitted His very life to those serving their own selfish desires. Very intentionally, God became weak on our account. This is the example that Paul follows. It is the example of humility and self-denial. And that is the example we are to walk in.

The Battle of Selves

The implication is that there is intentionality in denying self. We must live each day with the intention that we are going to be rooted in the truth of Christ.

As the journey through the desert reveals what you are clinging to, what human concerns you are drawing a sense of self from, it then becomes paramount to release your grip on those things. Putting the old self to death is a practice that takes time.

In his letter to the Galatians, Paul wrote that the flesh—the false self—wants what is contrary to the Spirit that lives within us, which is the source of our true self. Conversely, what the Spirit wants is contrary to the false self. There is a conflict between the old and new. Paul concludes that you are not simply to do what you want.[10] You are to test the source of your desires and emotions.

Spiritual growth is the process of denying more and more of who you are, like peeling back the layers of an onion. Your passion for yourself runs very deep. There are multiple layers to who you are and many things that are hidden within your heart. Paul wrote from experience about this process.

In the New Testament, we first meet Paul (called Saul at this time) as he was watching and approving the stoning of Stephen. As a show of respect for his power and position, those observing the proceedings laid their coats at the feet of Paul.[11] This gives us a clear picture of what was feeding Paul's false self. Who wouldn't be in love with that kind of affirmation?

After his conversion, we can move through Paul's writings according to the assumed order they were written, and see how his denial of self went deeper and deeper. In Galatians 2:6, Paul dismissed the other church leaders, saying, *"What they were makes no difference to me"* and that *"they added nothing to my message."* There was still pride in his sense of rightness.

Moving ahead in time a few years, when he wrote the first letter we have to the Corinthian church, he called himself "the least of the apostles."[12] In his perception of self, he had moved below those other leaders in status. Still a few years later, Paul released more of his grip and said that he is *"less than the least of all the Lord's people"*[13] Again, placing his sense of self below those he saved, not just the leaders. Finally, a couple years before his death, Paul referred to himself as the worst of all sinners.[14]

The more Paul saw himself in relation to God, the more he saw what he had in common with those for whom Christ died. These statements are not false modesty or self-criticism of performance. They are demonstrations that being a new creation in Christ is *active*. Putting the old self to death is a process of awareness.

All Christ followers eventually hit a wall in their spiritual growth. In time, growth may not come as fast as in a previous season because something deeply hidden must be confronted. Denying self cannot be faked with behavior modifications. Nor will going back to what was working previously allow you to move around or avoid this obstacle to growth.

As the new way becomes more difficult, people revert to old, comfortable patterns that seem familiar, are easier, and which have served them well before. Doing anything new feels awkward and takes intention.

If you have ever tried to adopt a new approach to eating, then this will give you a picture of what I'm talking about. You can stock the fridge with carrot chips and apples and whole grains, but you still have to choose those things when you open up the refrigerator door. It is usually pretty easy for enthusiasm to get you through the first couple days of a new dietary approach.

But at work you are going to be confronted with the vending machine, or maybe your driving route means you're going to pass by a favorite fast food place. Additionally, in times of stress, or when feeling depressed, or when you're out with friends and other similar situations, the temptation to go back to old behaviors will suddenly appear. You can know that those things are bad for you but at the same time they are familiar, comfortable, and provide a quick satisfaction. It takes a daily reminder of the bigger picture of your new eating habit to maintain success and overcome plateaus.

What Is Your Source of Faith?

Daily denying of self is faith being lived out. The author of the book of Hebrews said that faith is having the utmost confidence in what you hope for and an assurance about what you cannot see.[15] Faith is the denial of passion for self and affirmation of wholeness in God.

Being confident in what you hope for means developing awareness that your circumstances do not define your relationship with God. We live in a broken and fallen world where bad things happen. In this world, the creation itself is groaning for restoration, you encounter people pursuing wholeness apart from God, as well as other people who are working out their own identities in Christ. This has created broken systems and incomplete ways of relating. Judging the state of your relationship with God based on what is going on around you is misleading. Failures do not define you, nor do successes.

What you have done or will do is not who you are.
Who you know is not who you are.
How you are perceived is not who you are.

Faith is looking at your circumstances through the lens of Christ rather than looking at Christ through the lens of your circumstances. Faith is awareness of Whose you are. Becoming more and more aware of your brokenness and your tendencies, you will be able to choose differently—trusting the truth and goodness of God rather than choosing to believe the lie. Putting on the clothing of Christ in each moment by renewing your mind in the truth of who God is and who you are. That is a faith that transforms.

Surrendering Your Will

The heart—the Bible's word for our source of value—is a very complicated thing. Within the pages of the Bible, we are told two seemingly contradictory things about the heart.

First we learn that the heart is deceitful above all things.[16] Our pursuit of significance and acceptance will stop at nothing. We will lie, compare, teardown, steal, and do all sorts of other terrible things to ourselves and to others in the name of wholeness. These are the things that Jesus says defile us and pull us away from our true self.[17]

To Abraham's son Isaac, two sons were born. The oldest son was named Esau. As the oldest, he should have been the heir to the promise that God made to Abraham. It was his birthright, passed down from his father. One day, coming home from a long hunt, Esau was hungry. So hungry, in fact, that when his brother said he would only give Esau stew if he handed over his birthright, Esau did so with lust. Esau despised his God's promise.[18] This son of Isaac let hunger define him. His passion for self caused him to reject who God intended him to be. The heart of Esau was being deceitful above the main thing.

Elsewhere, we are also told that it is from the heart that life emanates.[19] From the previous chapter, we know that when we are rooted in Christ and immersed in the living water then the result is a life that is full, significant, meaningful and with purpose. This is why the heart must be guarded, and we need to be on the lookout for where it is rooted daily. This is our act of self-denial.

Because the heart is deceitful, it does not take too easily submitting to another. In his book *Desiring God's Will*, Dr. David Benner writes: "*Surrendering to God's will makes little sense if we are not first convinced of the depths of God's love for us. But surrender is far from complete and we have yet to unwrap the gift of our true-self-in-Christ until we are fully convinced of the absolute trustworthiness of God's will. Learning to prefer God's way to ours and discovering our identity and fulfillment in God's kingdom way demands that we know Love, deeply and personally. Only then will it be possible to choose God with the totality of our being, not just our will.*"[20]

Before any of us can surrender to God's will for our lives, we must live in a state of intentionally denying ourselves. It is not possible to serve two masters or keep one foot on each side of a fence.

In the garden as Jesus was praying he expressed his desire that there would be another cup from which He could drink from. Jesus was making one last plea, knowing the pain that was coming. Yet, after that moment He was resolute to let the Father's will be done, instead of His own will. Jesus was convinced of the Father's trustworthiness and love for Him. In that moment of stress and grief, Jesus made the choice to not live out of the flesh but out of his identity as the Son of God. Denial of self leads to purpose and obedience.

In one session with a client, I saw a man who decided that because his wife was not having sex with him and because her attention was focused more on the kids, he was therefore justified in leaving her for another woman. No amount of convincing of the selfishness of his stand nor of her willingness to own her mistakes would change his mind. His heart was deceitful above all things.

Denying self can take many forms. Internally, it means being aware of where our discontent is coming from. Is discontent coming from not having what you want when you want it? Is it simply impatience of false identity? Or is the discontent holy, wanting something that God is compelling you toward?

One is an act of pride and the other is an act of submission.

Walking In the Light

I am a very people-oriented person. I can read people's mannerisms well. Because I have had a lot of experience, I tend to understand a lot of what is going on inside people. The strength of this is the ability to communicate with, show compassion for, and provide help to people. The dark side is the ability to manipulate and use people in order to get what I want.

There are two sides to our strengths and our desires: a shadow side and a light side.

As you deny yourself and develop your identity in Christ, you will begin to act more and more out of the light side of the strength of who you are. There will be a period where there is ambivalence, not feeling bad about exercising your strength and yet not feeling good either. When you are so used to doing things to get what you want, finally using your strengths for God feels kind of murky.

After living so long fishing for compliments and craving for people to tell me good things, when I'm offered sincere praise I sometimes do not know how to respond. There is nothing wrong with being told good things; in fact all of us are to encourage one another. It took me some time to understand how not to let that become a source of significance again.

Once I left my job as a pastor, God rescued me and provided a job at a local university. The story of getting this job is a complete miracle, and an encouragement that God was not through with me yet. As I got used to my new surroundings and began to know the people I worked with, something interesting happened. Without prompting or telling them my background, they began to come to me for advice about dealing with the death of a loved one or conflict in a relationship. People were just drawn to talk to me. When I stopped using them to sustain my sense of self, my strengths shone forth on their own. God created influence in an environment to which I had unique access.

My client who felt like she needed to be the perfect wife began to experience something similar. As she let go of perfectionism and her demands for a positive response from her husband, she was able to become a more loving and patient wife. As she denied herself, she was ironically producing what she could not under her own selfish efforts. Of course, she still had to deal with the actions of her selfish husband (more on that in the next chapter), but she grew more and more to realize that his perceptions did not define who she was.

Being Watchful

Denying yourself daily requires constant watchfulness. *It is impossible to deny something of which you are not aware.* At times this can be overwhelming, and the temptation to just throw up your hands and say I'm never going to get it right can sometimes be strong. To say "I am too broken for God to use or too sinful for God to care about" is not denial; rather, that attitude is adopting brokenness as a way of life.

As you deny yourself and surrender to God's will, you will enter into freedom and rest. Often, freedom is misunderstood as autonomy or the ability to simply do what you want to do. Autonomy keeps you captive to the effectiveness of your own effort. Freedom comes from not having God as co-pilot, but giving Him the controls of the plane.

Gain Perspective

- Do you have a biblical character that speaks to you? What about that character resonates with your spiritual experience?

- What facet of Jesus' life and ministry does not mesh with your expectations of a Savior?

- How have you interpreted, understood, or been taught what "deny yourself" means?

- How does self-denial relate to your worth as a person?

- In what ways did Christ put on weakness?

- What obstacle to spiritual growth has the battle of selves produced in your life?

- Talk about the meaning of the statement: "Faith is looking at your circumstances through the lens of Christ rather than looking at Christ through the lens of your circumstances."

- How does your heart attempt to deceive you?

- A historical spiritual discipline is to use the "Jesus prayer" of Luke 18:13 as a way to meditate on denying self. Close your eyes, and for five minutes, slowly repeat "Lord Jesus Christ, have mercy on me, a sinner." How does this impact your mindset?

9

The Mystery of Faith

What is your cross?

During the height of my attempt to create a new life, I was cut off from my community. Aside from my parents and three other voices, I did not have any friends left. Terminating my relationship with my wife had been my choice; letting me go it alone was the choice of the community I had worked for.

When I had the Light shine in my eyes and I stepped on the path of repentance and awareness of my identity in Christ, my first natural reaction was to attempt to restore the relationships that had been strained. My actions had hurt a lot of people, so I took the intentional and humbling step of going to each of my co-workers and close friends and asking for forgiveness.

Beyond that, I pursued the resurrection of some of my friendships that had been dormant for those three long months. My initial hope was that some of the people with whom I had been close before would be interested in resuming our relationship. For reasons of their own, every case turned out to be impossible.

For a while I held onto the pain of this rejection. It was a challenge to my new sense of identity. I could hear the whisper of "If you were really doing things right, then these people would want to be your friends." It was hard to move forward in this circumstance.

In *Soulful Spirituality*, Dr. David Benner stated that "our natural reaction to any crisis, however, is to try and restore equilibrium."[1] This is the fight response to shame of putting the same pieces in the same places. Ronald Rolheiser differentiated between two types of life: the resuscitated life that is a return to a former state of health, and the resurrected life which is a transformation into something new.[2] I was on the path of resuscitation.

Since God is the Author, He intervened. It turned out that He was guiding me into something new. My tendency was to cling to what was old and familiar. I was trying to put new wine into old wine skins. In this situation, God taught me the first lesson of the spiritual life. Pruning of some unhealthy things was necessary for new life to bloom.

This is a principle of nature, and it is the truth of biblical spirituality: death precedes new life.

Carrying Your Cross

In the previous chapter, we started to examine Christ's instruction regarding what a follower of His must do. It began with a denial of self. What comes next is the need to carry one's cross.[3] While in Christ we are citizens of heaven, the present reality is that each of us are still inhabitants of this broken world. Carrying a cross is the burden in this world that we must carry, as our life is surrendered to Him.

As you are transformed into the likeness of Jesus, relational, economic, and cultural systems will press against you in an effort to get you to live your life the old way.

Your spouse is still going to have their same annoying habits. There are still going to be bills to pay and desires to deal with as you spend and earn money. Your drive for sex is still going to be low or high. There may be an unfulfilled desire for a child or you may have a child that is strong-willed. Longings and desires are still going to be part of your life, and as the Benner quote above alludes to, there is going to be a pull to satisfy them in known ways. In Christ, you also will still have to live with and deal with the consequences to broken decisions and behaviors of your past. This does not mean you are not forgiven, just that every action has ripples of effect. Jesus is One who experienced suffering, frustration, anger, disappointment, hurt, rejection, and physical wounds, and He can empathize with you as you walk the path in His steps.

The good news is that Christ is present to carry your cross alongside you. Your burden in Him will be light because your source of worth and perception of self is no longer rooted in these old things.[4]

Very often there is the expectation communicated directly or subtly that the moment you begin to follow Christ, everything will instantaneously change. The myth is that being in Christ means all the pain and hurt will go away. But, when the reality of pain continues, we make the assumption that we must be doing something wrong.

In truth, much does change—you are enabled by the spirit living within you, there is peace with God, and access to unlimited grace and forgiveness. But there are addictions to face and behaviors to unlearn. While the circumstances of your life are going to be the same as they were, you are new. Your new identity gives you the ability to overcome and to respond differently.

Some suffering you face is going to be due to those circumstances you are already in. There are parts of your life you will have to learn to live with, just as Jacob learned to live with the limp he got when wrestling with God.[5] Paul was told that Christ's grace was sufficient as he dealt with a thorn in the flesh.[6] Was his thorn a physical issue or one of desire? While we are not told, Christ's offer of grace leads me to believe this was something that tempted Paul to avert his eyes from Christ. Even though Paul was an apostle, this irritation was still part of his spiritual life.

Other suffering amounts to dealing with and letting go of the longing for the way things were. As the Israelites were led by Moses to step into their freedom, they still had to deal with hunger that was insufficiently satisfied and thirst from being in the hot desert.

The nation looked back to their mud huts and meat in their pots with longing. Then they grumbled and complained, and accused Moses of leading them into the desert so that they could die of thirst. *They yearned for slavery!* Even though they were beginning to step into their identity as the people of God, they needed to learn how to carry their burden.

The Death of the Old

Loss and death is a part of every aspect of this life. In God's economy, nothing is wasted. In fact, the promise made to His followers is that in all things God is working for our good. The good is not the resolution of circumstances in your favor, but that you would be shaped in the image of His Son.[7] Biblically, this is the pattern that God uses to create in us new life. Death and loss lead to transformation and new life.

A few examples will help to see this pattern. Joseph, with the identity of the favored son, was thrown into a well by his brothers. Assumed to be dead, Joseph lost everything: status, wealth, and relationships. Yet, as the story of Joseph unfolds, you will see a man that grows in dependence upon God and rejects the false familial sources of identity.

Jonah's identity was entrenched in the superiority of the nation Israel. In order to escape the plan of God that was messing with his sense of self, Jonah asked to be thrown from the side of a ship. While sinking, he was swallowed by an enormous fish and spit back out—a foreshadowing of Christ's resurrection—on dry land. Jonah was still a work in progress, but God was not giving up.

Because they sought identity elsewhere, the entire nation of Israel was defeated and sent into Babylon. Again, this death of an entire nation's existence would lead to their ultimate spiritual good and preparation to receive the Messiah.

Finally, Jesus presents the most significant picture. His death on the cross was the death to our old way of living, and His resurrection was the enabling of our peace with the Creator and our ability to have access to His image. The church father Augustine labeled this pattern of death leading to new life as the "paschal mystery". Paschal means passing, as in, just prior to the exodus from Egypt, the paschal lamb whose blood caused God to pass over the houses of those who offered a sacrifice out of trust.[8]

Christ is our Passover offering. The final Paschal lamb, His blood allows us to shed the self-made clothes of death and experience freedom and new life. Jesus appearing in the flesh to take our punishment on Himself and being raised from the dead is the mystery of our faith.[9] There can be no resurrection without the cross.

Without suffering and loss, there will be no refining of your faith.[10]

Part of the Paschal Mystery is that we must let go of the old in order to experience new life. The theological term for this is sanctification; your identity becoming more aligned with the true self of who you are in Christ. You reach greater maturity as you come to understand all that Chist offered. God gave us everything He had.

Sanctification is achieved by living a pattern of death and resurrection. Author Ron Rolheiser speaks of the pattern of the Paschal Mystery as the fear and confusion and pain of Good Friday, the experience of grief and hopelessness and despair of Holy Saturday, and the new life and the joy of Easter Sunday.

Letting Go

Mary Magdalene was among the first to find the empty tomb of Jesus. When she arrived there was someone there who she perceived to be a gardener, and so she conversed with him. Her expectations of who Jesus was kept her from seeing Him before her. At the point that Jesus revealed Himself to her, her first response gives a clue to her mindset, for she called Him teacher.

Then she grabbed hold of Jesus, which He graciously allowed. This was an expression of her expectation that everything was going to be as it was before. Jesus told her to let go of Him, not because He was uncomfortable with intimacy, but to teach Mary that there was going to be a new order to things. In order for there to be new life, Mary had to let go of her old image of who Jesus was.

Finding life means that you must let go of who you want, or who you think you need Jesus to be. Before you can step into new life, you must confront the false images and grieve how they become part of your life.

The same pattern is a part of how we deal with circumstances as well. God's first choice for king of Israel had been a failure. Saul chose to put his identity in the power and wealth of being king rather than surrendering to the God who had chosen him. When God moved on from Saul, the prophet Samuel kept his eyes focused on the past.

Finally, God confronted Samuel and asked, "How long will you mourn for Saul, since I have rejected him as king over Israel?"[11] This attitude of looking back and wanting things to remain the same kept Samuel from looking forward to the hope of a new king after God's own heart.

Letting go will be an act of frustration if there is not simultaneously something else to grab onto. And not just substituting one false source of worth for another. Grab onto hope in Christ. When Zacchaeus was called by Jesus, it changed what he was grabbing onto in life. Rather than wealth, by seeking worth in the God who noticed him in the tree, Zacchaeus was able to give half over everything he had to the poor without hesitation. In order to make amends, he also promised to pay back four times anyone he had cheated.[12] This is the power of letting go of the old self.

Back to my own experience, I needed God's guidance because I could not hold onto relationships in their old format. My relational pattern was to be the pursuer, and it was unhealthy for me to be the one always chasing a relationship. I had been the one who became what other people needed. If I was going to live in truth, this required a new way for me to experience friendship that required a letting go of the old. If I truly grasped that God loved me, then I also needed to believe that I was worth being given equal effort in a relationship. This wasn't a process I expected or understood at the beginning, and that was how God and his Spirit led me through.

Holy Saturday

Imagine being a follower of Jesus who witnessed His arrest and crucifixion. Good Friday was filled with confusion and fear as preconceived notions of a messiah were shattered. Easter Sunday was a day where hope took a new form and purpose was restored as the message spread that Jesus was alive and He said to go to Galilee. But what of Saturday?

Holy Saturday was a day where the shock wore off as the disciples awoke to the reality of Christ's death. Grief and mourning were the primary emotions, but also hopelessness and despair as seemingly everything the disciples had invested in was taken away. For us, as we live in the cycle of death and resurrection, we must learn to move through Saturday.

There is a grieving process that is necessary with letting go of the old. "Good grieving, however, consists not just in letting the old go but also in letting it bless us."[13] Like Mary in the garden, and Saul relating to the king, there must be an intentional release in order to be blessed. Before I could return to ministry, develop a coaching framework, or write this book, I had to make the step of releasing and being blessed by my old relationships and habits. Too often though, we attempt to experience relief, which keeps the work of God from happening. Instead of grieving, you may be substituting the strategy of trying to forget.

The grief of the false self resents others while godly grief forgives. While the false self will make penance to try to fight shame, godly grief repents secure in its value. The grief of the false self looks backward with regret, leading to bitterness. A good example is Lot's wife as God pulls them from the city they were living in.[14] The godly grief of Holy Saturday looks forward to restoration.

Don't confuse grief with avoidance or stuffing it away. Anything that you avoid will eventually come back to the surface. *When we fail to mourn properly our incomplete lives, then this incompleteness becomes a gnawing restlessness, a bitter center that robs our lives of all delight.*[15]

One of the people that I have worked with has some relationships that were unhealthy. These were friendships that were destructive and did not bring a sense of life into my client's world. When we talked about evaluating those relationships and whether they should be pruned, there was a lot of resistance. A lot of fear surrounded this decision because this person felt like even though they weren't great friendships, they at least kept them from being lonely. Better to have these people than no people at all was the reasoning.

The amazing thing that God did was that when this person had the strength of character and belief in their value as someone living in the image of God and did prune these negative relationships, God was able to fill the new margin in life with healthy spiritual friendships. Once they stopped looking back with regret, he was able to move forward with forgiveness and experience new life.

The death of the old preceded new life.

The Dark Night

Sometimes, carrying our cross will beat us into a dark night of the soul. We can get stuck in Saturday and experience a sense of desolation where we struggle to grasp the presence of God. *"These are feelings that you will notice if you prayerfully attend to what happens in your depths when you turn away from God."*[16] Desolation feels like a downward spiral of agitation and apprehension in our relationship with God. It can be brought about when we focus on what we are lacking, or how far we have yet to go, or when we feel the shame of taking a step backward—losing focus and looking at God through the lens of circumstances. It is a stumble along the path as we carry our cross.

Just as Jesus stumbled three times when he was carrying his cross, there will be times when you will stumble. No one will be perfect in this process. Failures are an opportunity to learn. Such times are the reason that followers are to carry one another's burdens.[17] Jesus received help carrying His cross; there will be people in your life that you have to allow to carry the burden with you. Admitting that you need help and don't have all the answers is part of the life of a believer in Christ. Knowing your limitations is humility.

From humility comes the ability to express self-compassion— being able to accept that you are imperfect, and live in a broken world. Being able to look at yourself and accept your limitations without a corresponding loss of perceived value—to remember that your identity is not based on your performance or perfection. If Christ forgives us, then you should have the ability to move past regret and offer yourself the grace you'd give others.

Stepping Into the New

Is it possible to experience the new life without releasing the old?

In chapter 5, we briefly looked at Jesus' statement that in order to be his disciple you had to hate your father and mother, wife and children, and brothers and sisters. This meant that to follow Jesus means to no longer seek affirmation and worthiness from lesser sources. Your family system may still be the cross that you have to bear, but it no longer defines you.

I have related to you several different aspects of my client who tried to be perfect in her marriage, and that ultimately came from a family system that reinforced the notion that nothing she did was good enough. Even while working on her identity and letting freedom get a foothold, she still had to bear the burden of a mother who was demanding and thankless. My client's responses to her mother could now be different, but her mother was still part of her life. It was the cross she had to bear.

But it could just as easily be said that…

- If you do not hate your busyness, then you cannot be His disciple.

- If you do not hate your appearance, then you cannot be His disciple.

- If you do not hate your bank account, then you cannot be His disciple.

- If you do not hate your Facebook 'likes,' then you cannot be His disciple.

- If you do not hate your _____, then you cannot be His disciple.

All of these things are a reality of life that you will still interact with, but no longer will you have to look to them in order to define who you are. They are your cross, and sanctification means releasing your grip and allowing Christ to bear more and more of the weight of the burden.

Jesus applied this principle to His followers with these words recorded by John: *"Very truly I tell you, unless a kernel of wheat falls to the ground and dies, it remains only a single seed. But if it dies, it produces many seeds."*[18] New life requires death or loss; it requires that we reject the standards of this world and carry that burden through life. Doing so multiplies influence, blessing, and freedom.

As you develop your identity in Christ and experience change, the reality of relational systems is that they will change as well. But this does not always mean for the better because others will try to cling on to what they have always had. As you learn new, healthy behaviors, you may withdraw the sense of worth you had been providing to others. Then you'll experience their "fight, flight, or freeze" shame response. Sometimes things have to get worse before they can get better. There may be suffering and trials due to the fact that you are no longer dependent on other people and other roles for your sense of self.

I still do friendship, fatherhood, and marriage imperfectly. But I am able to more and more rest in the fact that I am worth loving for who I am, rather than for what I produce or what I can give another person. Rather than always being the one who pursues relationship and sets up time to get together, I allow people for space to pursue me. This is how I carry my cross.

Gain perspective

- Which pattern do you live in: resuscitation or resurrection?

- How would you fill in the blank: if I do not hate _____, I cannot be Jesus' disciple. Explain.

- How does what you filled in the blank keep you from practicing the presence of God?

- What endings or pruning do you need to make in order to have the space to step into the new life God has for you?

- Who helps you carry your cross?

10 | Following Jesus

How do you develop a good root?

I spent some time consulting with and working in a denomination that practiced Lent every year. For those who don't know, Lent is the forty or so days leading up to the celebration of Jesus' resurrection. Traditionally, something meaningful is given up during Lent as a way to experience sacrifice and lack.

As a kid raised Catholic, I grew up with Lent. My family would give up desserts, and as kids, we would groan and complain and tell anyone who would listen just how much of a sacrifice we were making not getting to have chocolate or ice cream. Some people carry that same attitude into the entirety of their relationship with Christ.

The spiritual intent of Lent is turning away from something that gives you a sense of comfort, security, or control (a few years ago I stopped looking at my blog stats). Instead of boasting and finding a sense of righteousness in the act of giving something up, it should be used as a time to remove barriers and draw near to God.

When Jesus teaches about spiritual practices like fasting, charity, and prayer, He makes the point not to do such things for an audience.[1] By putting your righteous acts on display for affirmation, you are doing them for your benefit rather than out of pursuit of God. As is the case with Lent, *all spiritual disciplines are for the purpose of self-examination and developing intimacy with God.*

In the past couple chapters, we have examined Jesus' words about what it takes to be his disciple. First you must deny your false sense of self; second, you must be ready to carry the burden of brokenness, and finally, you are to follow Him.[2] When Luke related this same teaching in his writings, he added the word 'daily'.[3] Following Jesus is not something that you do once in a while, or compartmentalize into certain parts of your life and not others. Being a follower is a way of life, seeping into every moment—all of your decisions, behaviors, and relationships will be affected.

Following Jesus is about nurturing and developing your root. The case has been made throughout this book that your decisions, behaviors, and ways you relate to others are a product of where your identity is rooted. What comes out of your heart is what has the ability to make you unclean, because bad fruit comes from an identity that is disconnected from the Father.[4] Decisions, behaviors, and relationships are consistent with your root.

The Rhythm of Life

Nurturing your root takes practice and care. The soil where your root is planted must be watered and provided nutrients, and just like a plant, you must be kept in the light. It is God that makes things grow, but you are responsible for the conditions.[5] When you are not intentionally aware of your roots, you become like one who is tossed about by different wise-sounding beliefs and opinions.

It is very helpful to develop what in ancient Christian spirituality was called a 'rule of life'. A rule is not a law; it is a framework of incorporating spiritual practices into the moments of the day so that you will not get sidetracked by people or circumstances, and lose focus on your identity in Christ.[6]

Because to our ears the word rule brings images of legalism, I prefer the term 'rhythm of life'. It is likely that your life is already lived in some sort of rhythm. There is a pattern to your typical day. Awake at 6:00 am, breakfast for the kids at 6:30, and leave the house by 7:30 to be at work by eight. Some rhythm provides the structure for a usual day. Even looking at the week as a whole, there can be a pattern. In my house, because we are all tired at the end of the week, my family has adopted 'frozen pizza Friday' as a way to take the focus off preparing dinner and put it on us having some family time. For us, this has become part of our rhythm of life.

A rule of life is not about observing a set schedule or to-do list in order to make yourself good and acceptable before God. Also, it is not something that is static; as you grow and change, so will your rhythm.

Developing a rhythm is not about adding to your busyness. Rather, it is about choosing to draw near to God.

Does that sound impossible? Is the first thought that crashes into your mind an objection as to why you do not have time to develop spiritual disciplines? Then go back through the last two chapters, which talk about denying your false self and taking up your cross in the midst of life's circumstances, and examine the root of the objection. God will not take a backseat to lesser things[7], and this is really where the rubber meets the road in your spiritual life.

Here we find the meaning of Jesus' parable of the farmer who sows seeds. In the story, the seed is spread on four types of soil. The path that is packed down, rocky soil, weed overgrown soil, and prepared soil. In His explanation[8], Jesus relates each of the soils to one's source of worth.

The path represents the person whose identity has no room for Jesus. Truth cannot make an impact on the heart that is hard. Rocky soil is described as the identity that does not develop root. This is the person who remains captive to their lies, and hence, is uprooted easily. In the overgrown soil, identity in Christ is choked out by the concerns of the world. The false self dominates. But the soil that has been prepared diligently, the good soil, allows the truth of God to take root. God has made himself knowable, and it is up to you to choose to be known by Him.

Practicing the Disciplines

Spiritual disciplines are the pursuit of intimacy with your Creator. Practice makes perfect is the old saying, so practice in spiritual disciplines will cause the clothing of Christ that we wear to not feel awkward and unfamiliar, but as a second skin with which we engage naturally.

A genuine spiritual discipline is an act of love offered to God with no strings attached.[9] You humbly open yourself before God as a response to his acceptance of you. Disciplines are an act of giving not to get back, but because God has made Himself the source of who you are.

It is so important to heed the caution that spiritual disciplines are not a way to be like God—that is the Lie—or to prove your worth, but instead, are a way to be open to Him and to express to Whom your life belongs.

What follows is not an exhaustive list of disciplines, but a way to get started. There are many fantastic books on spiritual disciplines[10] and I have taken the liberty to describe some practices that are less commonly taught, but can be amazingly transforming.

The discipline of solitude. Life in our culture is filled with noise and distraction. There is constant input. We try to fill ourselves up with our phones and entertainment and busyness. Anything, it seems, to avoid the stream of thoughts, doubts, and questions that pervade our conscious mind. More and more, our minds are becoming undisciplined and the response is to drown it out.

Isolation is not the same as solitude. When you isolate yourself, you are removed from a relationship physically or in some other manner, but you still are ignoring your thoughts and God. Recently, the radio in my car broke and I have been using my earphones while driving. Because I tend to be in the middle of listening to something, I have been keeping them in when I get out of the car and walking to the office. A few days ago, the realization struck me—what an easy way to be isolated. With earphones in I am no longer responsive to the people around me, nor am I receptive to new inputs. It is a way to hide in plain sight.

Solitude is intentionally taking the time to put the noise, clutter, and demands of life to the side. The purpose is twofold: you can quiet your mind and control your thoughts, and then make yourself available to God. Here is what you will find when you first practice solitude—your mind will race because it is not used to slowing down. Things to do, negative thoughts, and memories will begin to bubble to the surface. You must let them float by—do not grab onto them. What works for me is to picture those thoughts as if they are floating on a stream I'm standing in, and I use my hands to move them past me.

On more than one occasion, Jesus abandoned the crowds and His disciples in order to go to a solitary place and pray.[11] He disengaged from the demands and expectations in order to be alone with the Father. Setting aside time to be with the Father ought to be the most regular discipline. What you do with your time, which we have all been given an equal daily amount of, is a demonstration of choosing Him over other things.

It seems like a good time to say that solitude can be practiced differently by different people. Some will need to find a quiet room, others will want to be outside, or in a church. Context is not important; what you set the time aside for is. Follow your path in each of these disciplines, not the path or expectations of others. God has made you in a unique way, so practicing these ways of opening up may look different in your life than others. Likewise, He knows how He made you and will be faithful to meet you when you set aside time for Him.

The discipline of confession. For the false self, true confession is virtually impossible. Unless confessing is the lesser of two evils or will add clout to the false identity, your pride will avoid it. The reason is that admitting fault takes away value and exposes shame. In order to turn away from something and confess it to another, your foundation of worth must be secure and unchanging.

Practicing confession as a discipline means keeping an eye on your own brokenness and realizing that you are loved by God, not for your performance but because He created you. One of the lies that you will be tempted to believe is that in Christ you are better than others. It is easy to forget from where you came as you live in your grace-filled state in Christ. The willingness to say I am sorry to God and to others, without simultaneously feeling devalued or shamed, is an act of humility.

In recovery groups, there is a priority on having a sponsor. This is someone that can be turned to when there is a sense that the old thoughts and temptations are creeping back in. In the same way, followers of Jesus are told to confess their sins to one another.[12] Sin thrives in secrecy because it feeds on the feeling that no one else has done this.

Confession is not a way for each of us to hold one another in check. Hearing another's confession is not about power in a relationship, although there can be the ability to improperly use what is known. An act of intimacy, speaking your sin aloud to another shines light on the sin and takes its power away. With fear no longer present, the confessor can then focus on reconnecting with the image of God.

When you hear another's confession of disconnection, avoid the temptation to prescribe a fix unless that is what is being asked for. Usually, when someone gets to the point of admitting wrong, they know what needs to change.

The discipline of forgiveness. As with confession, the false sense of self finds it difficult to offer forgiveness because wrongs against you are challenging your sense of worth, acceptance, and security. The debt is too large to be released.

Debt is the language that Jesus uses when talking about forgiveness. When teaching the disciples to pray, Jesus told them to ask God to "forgive us our debts, as we also have forgiven our debtors,"[13] and in His parable about forgiveness, Jesus uses the example of a king who forgave the debts of all his servants, yet there was one who refused to release an infinitely smaller debt.[14]

Being *complete* with your identity rooted in Christ, debts against you can be released. In fact, the parable mentioned in the previous paragraph alludes to the liberalness with which you are to offer forgiveness. You lose nothing by forgiving other people because your identity is secure on the rock solid foundation of Christ.

A word of caution: as you apply the Paschal Mystery and grieve the debts against you and allow the light of Christ to fill in those deficits, that does not necessarily mean everything goes back to being the way it was or the way you hoped it would be. Reconciliation may be possible, but if the other person refuses to acknowledge the wrong or will not change, reconciliation may not be possible nor wise.

The discipline of gratitude. During the exodus from the slavery of Egypt, the Israelites continually grumbled and complained about what they did not have, despite being a community of free people of whom God had taken ownership. Because of this, God labeled the Israelites a *stiff-necked people.* Their necks were stiff because they focused down on themselves rather than looking up to God. Being stiff-necked was a description of their ingratitude.

Gratitude is being mindful of what is good in your life.[15] Looking for where God is at work may start with being thankful everyday for the grace that you have received and will receive. Regardless of your circumstance, you are in Christ and that does not change. There may be times when that is all you are able to be thankful for. Developing a mindset of gratitude may also mean looking to a sunset, design of nature, the change in you, or the growth of your spouse, and recognizing God's work. Gratitude is a discipline, and continual ingratitude may be a symptom of an area of your life that is disconnected from God.

The discipline of generosity. Because God has given you a new identity that is not dependent upon what you have, you have the ability to release your grip on the money and things that once provided status and significance. Being generous means seeing the needs of others, their humanity, and in Whose likeness they have been made and sharing. Looking past what they can produce or provide, you are to find ways to serve others. Much like prayer, your giving is not to be on display for others to see, or else it may become a source of righteous feelings.[16]

In looking out for the needs of others, you are abandoning benefit to yourself. The discipline of giving will be a reminder of your dependence upon God and trust in His promise to provide everything you need to live.

For the Jewish people, generosity was demonstrated through giving of more than just money and things, but more importantly for them was giving time and talent. Even if you do not have much to spare financially, you can find ways to be generous. Without giving of yourself, opening your wallet can become a way to hide.

An incredibly humbling side note about generosity is found in the book of Proverbs. God so identifies with the poor, marginalized, and those in need, that He says that when you give to them you are lending to Him.[17] Let this truth sink in. Not only has God given you everything He has, He is willing to go into your debt when you are generous with others. Practice this discipline!

The discipline of play. Growing up, children are encouraged to play. Doing so boosts imagination, is healthy for the body, and it is a healthy way to interact with others. Yet, as adults, play is either completely abandoned or becomes a preoccupation. Even in many of the things done for recreation, like golf, running, knitting, etc., there is competition or perfectionism. In that case, what you are doing is no longer fun but for a goal or sense of worth.

When was the last time you've had a good laugh? What was the last activity you engaged in without considering its productivity or your performance?

One highly motivated client confided in me that he does not do anything for fun. His life is all business and no play, and it was wearing him down. Together, we spent a session exploring things he would like to do or try, and also why he had stopped playing. It was all tied up with his sense of self and being productive. Play releases stress and allows the mind to open up and relax. Knowing this, my client regretted abolishing hobbies from his life.

Sometimes we make the excuse that we are enjoying our vocation so much, we're just going to do it all the time. Yet, while we may be able to convince ourselves of that for a time, for our brains, that is not the truth. In the book *Play*, Stuart Brown says that we were built for play, and the ability to engage in such times of play is critical not only for happiness, but also for sustaining social relationships, being creative, and being innovative.[18]

The discipline of truth. God is the source of truth. Your opinions are not the standard of truth, nor are your feelings a benchmark of truth. Both of those things can potentially be based in truth, but they are not sources.

There are two areas from which truth can be discerned. First, we are given a general truth that is available to everyone when they look at the world around them.[19] Second, there is the truth revealed to us in the Bible.

Interacting with what is true and hiding the truth in your heart so that it becomes a part of your identity is an essential discipline. It is part of the process of renewing your mind. The scriptures are something with which you must continually be engaged. There are different ways to pursue this interaction.

Reading the Bible is a good place to start. But, you must avoid reading the Bible for information as you would a textbook. Rather, the Bible should be read for transformation. Quality of reading takes priority over quantity. For this reason, I'm not a big fan of "in a year" goals for reading the Bible because then the mindset becomes to 'get it done' rather than allow the truth to seep into you.

Contemplation is a good way to practice the discipline of truth. Taking a verse or passage and savoring it, reading it repeatedly and slowly. Praying through the words and allowing God to speak. When coupled with writing down responses, questions or application to your present circumstance, this is a powerful way to practice the truth.

Imaginative reading is also a powerful tool. Putting yourself into a scene or story and imagining what you are seeing, feeling, smelling, and hearing can cause you to gain a new perspective on a passage. Taking time to study the Bible is also important. Books and passages cannot be separated from their context. Knowing the audience and what kind of writing a particular chapter or book is will give deeper insight into the application of truth. Undoubtedly, you have a particular way you like to engage with the Bible. But don't focus on one facet at the expense of others. There are seasons for contemplation, reading, and study; make the most of every opportunity.

Usually, when reference is made to hiding the truth of the word in the heart[20], the implication is that it should be memorized. Again, memorization can be a good thing, but it is also possible to have knowledge without being touched by or applying it. But the verse speaking of hiding the word in your heart goes beyond memorization; it is letting the truth become the core of who you are and the way you see yourself and God. Then you will remain connected to Him and not to sin.

The discipline of pruning. Where I live, orange trees are in abundance. At the end of each picking season, the farmers have a machine that trims the top of the trees and gives them a flat top. The effect is that these orange trees grow taller and fuller and bear more fruit because of the pruning. Other trees are like that too, but every year, I marvel at the flat uniformity of the tree line in the healthy groves.

In the previous chapter, I talked about pruning as part of the Paschal Mystery. Pruning is tough and painful. But in evaluating your spiritual life and connection to God, part of the process is looking out at what or who keeps you from staying connected to His image.

Are you living simply? Part of living in the newness of life may involve adopting a more frugal lifestyle and avoiding the trappings of keeping up with the Joneses. Fasting is a facet of the frugality and pruning.

Are your environments and relationships spurring your towards Christ? In his book *Necessary Endings*, Dr. Henry Cloud says that there are always going to be environments and relationships in your life that you can classify as healthy, healthy but using resources that could better be used elsewhere, unhealthy and dying, and dead.[21]

It would be great if all decisions were between good and bad things. The probability of making healthy decisions might increase.

But, some decisions are between good things and better things. This is the situation in which you have a healthy relationship or environment, but your time, energy, and resources could have had more impact elsewhere. So if the choice is between staying at the office and taking your child to soccer, which do you prune?

Those that are dying or dead are those that take energy away from you and dissipate joy, and inhibit you from seeing in God. In one way or another, those things need to be pruned. Pruning may be as dramatic as getting rid of that environment or relationship from your life. Thus,

- A toxic friendship may need to take another form or be let go.

- A marriage that is in disrepair may be in need of renewed emotional commitment and pursuit of professional help. It may be time to assess and develop boundaries, pruning the unhealthy ways of relating or being related to.

- You may need to stop working the extra hours for that new car. Even still, maybe the desire for that new car has to go, and you'll have to drive an older car so you can devote more time and resources to God.

- You may need to find a job that gives you opportunity to excel.

It is vital that you intentionally and regularly look at the aspects of life that need to be fostered and need to be pruned.

How often do you say "no" to demands on your time? On the one hand, you are probably very busy, but on the other, you suffer from guilt or anxiety that you are letting someone down. For church leaders and those active in church work, it is tempting to use the lie that you need to say yes because you are building the kingdom of God. Truth is, it is God's kingdom and your first priority is to be rooted in Christ. That is an issue of identity.

It might be possible that "no" is a word that needs to be added to your vocabulary. An alternative to busyness is being unhurried.

An unhurried pace of life is a purposeful use of time; an attitude of discernment about your capabilities and why you are saying "yes" or "no" to something. Ten times out of ten, I'd rather someone give me an honest "no" than tell me "yes" and either resent me or not follow through.

What opportunities have presented themselves in your life that you have been just too busy to pursue? Has someone offered friendship? Have you been asked to mentor or build someone up? Without a focus on maintaining space in your life, you will miss out on opportunities to use your talents and abilities, thus substituting busyness for the greater good of the kingdom.

The discipline of celebration. God is a Celebrator. In His commands to the Israelites, there were many opportunities for feasts and rest. These were to be times celebrating the protection and provision of God. Celebrating was an expression of trust and thankfulness.

The kingdom of heaven is compared to a wedding banquet.[22] The words that Jesus promises to those who have been faithful are "well done."[23] Celebration is important.

When was the last time you took the time to celebrate an accomplishment or a milestone?

Your Act of Worship

Worship is the act of finding your significance in something, or being defined by it. These disciplines are intended to help you grow deeper and deeper in understanding Jesus as that source. Surrendering your identity to God and being defined by His love for you is your spiritual act of worship. In that way you will become a living sacrifice as you follow the example of Christ.

As you read over these disciplines, or consider others from the resources that have been recommended, here is a word of advice.

Do not overwhelm yourself.

There might be the temptation to believe if a little is good, then more is better. The only problem with that thinking is that gradual, lasting change is better than burning out and making no change. If you were to decide today that you wanted to train for a half-marathon, you would not get off the couch, put on running shoes, and gallop ten miles. You would consider your present physical state as you picked a place to start. That may involve running a half mile today and building up.

Consider your present spiritual state and try something. Maybe it is substituting fifteen minutes of solitude each day for something else. Or contemplating a verse for ten minutes. Or choosing to prune one item from your busy schedule. Remember, you are walking your own path. Avoid comparison and practice celebration.

Be persistent. Don't try something one time only; give it a few days to see how it fits. If what you try feels like a chore or obligation, try something new. Connecting to your source should bring life and freedom.

Also, you can try different disciplines in different contexts and rhythms. Some things might be a daily discipline. Other practices might be weekly or monthly. For the example of solitude, while I like to have a daily time to myself for contemplation and prayer, I also plan a quarterly time to take a night away and just pray, read the Bible, listen, and journal. This is part of my rhythm, and I share it to show how a discipline can have different contexts.

As you are starting, don't develop an intense schedule. Start small. The more you do these things, the more you will want to do them. The more you practice discipline, the easier it will become, and the more you'll sense God's presence in them. That is the ultimate way to fill yourself.

Taste and see that the LORD IS GOOD;
blessed is the one who takes refuge in him.

Psalm 34:8

Gain Perspective

- What is the difference between choosing not to sin and choosing to remain open to God?

- Describe the general rhythm of your typical day. Where are there gaps or busyness?

- Who is the person in your life that you confess your sins to? How do you avoid the temptation of the false self to gloss over your sins?

- Who in your life are you still expecting to pay a debt to you?

- Name one thing for which you are grateful.

- After an initial reading, what discipline mentioned seems to resonate with you? How can you incorporate that into your rhythm of life tomorrow?

Part Four
The Fruit

*By this everyone will know that you are my disciples,
if you love one another.*

John 13:35

11

Not Meant to Be Alone

How do you love others well?

As the second chapter of Mark's gospel opens, we encounter four men who were carrying their paralyzed friend on a mat with the hope of seeing Jesus.[1] You can just hear the shuffle of their feet on the sand and the sweat dripping down on all their faces. Yet they were excited because after trying to help their friend in every way they could, they realized that Jesus was the only way through which their friend would be whole again.

So they loaded him onto a carpet, each grabbing a corner, and they walked however far they needed to bring their friend into the presence of the Healer. Suffering with another is an act of compassion. But who says loving is easy? When they got to the house where Jesus was speaking, there were thousands of people surrounding it. At this point they could have turned to each other, said *not this time*, and rationalized that maybe He'll get around their area again. Instead, these friends were undeterred and pushed through the crowd, climbed on top of the house and dug a hole in the roof.

All with a full-grown man on a mat! Nothing was going to stop their mission of love.

While we are not told so in the story, I'm sure they knew that they would have to compensate the owner of the house for this intrusion. Maybe the cost would be in the form of money or time for labor, but in order to love their friend those obstacles were insignificant. This story is a picture of love that every follower of Christ is to demonstrate regularly. Love counts the cost and moves forward anyway. In order to love others well, you are required to lay down your life for them.[2]

When you are open to God and have your identity firmly rooted in His truth, only then can you truly love others without thought of self. Because you no longer need fulfillment from others, nor are you in competition with them for identity resources, you can actively work toward relieving their suffering and burdens. In this way you join in Christ's ministry of reconciliation.[3]

What Keeps You from Loving Well

Depending upon relationships for a sense of acceptance and worth will keep you from truly loving others. In that case, your actions will be based on a foundation centered on self: to get the security, control, or affirmation that your false sense of self needs.

A very cultural example is the man who will say anything to a woman he is trying to sleep with. In such a view, his investment in the relationship is for a perceived benefit to self. But, this principle can be demonstrated in many other ways.

It is demonstrated by the pastor who will always say yes because he or she wants to be seen as a saver. Another example is the spouse who lays on the guilt when the other wants to have a night out with friends. This pattern is also observed in a friend who tears another down or gossips in order to gain acceptance. You can probably fill in an example based on what you do or what has been done to you.

When relationship is a source of wholeness, the humanity is taken away from the other. The person simply becomes a means to an end, and the relationship is approached as a pragmatic tool.

The result is expectations, manipulation, control, and comparison all based on what is best for you.

As I have confessed before in the pages of this book, I looked to my wife to give me a sense of affirmation and worthiness. Her happiness was the barometer of how good of a person I was. Hence, my behaviors and decisions in the relationship were an attempt to prove my competence. So I cleaned the house every week because that was something a 'good husband' would do, but resented having to do it. I also allowed my wife to make the financial decisions, again as a way to be seen as good. All I wanted was her approval, and the benefits that I hoped might follow.

On the outside, my actions looked as if they were loving. But under the surface, they were rooted in self. In order to describe this, Jesus used the analogy of a burial tomb painted a bright, clean white. Things looked good on the outside, but inside there was decay and death. Each day, when I left the house it was with a smile on my face and a commitment to never reveal my frustrations of feelings of inadequacy to a small group or a friend. Like the Pharisees of whom Jesus used the white-washed tomb description, I was full of self-indulgence and hypocrisy.[4]

Rather than people to be loved, others become objects that produce value within us. Compounding the problem is the fact that these "objects" also have identities and quests for significance that they are following. In addition to being dissatisfied by what we receive from each other, the shame cycle is unleashed as we are forced to confront our own inadequacy in sustaining another's identity.

The false way of relating places stress on others. Whether that is in the demands we place on another in order to make us feel valued or whether it is competing with them so that we can find security or control, this impacts our ability to love. Another person was not meant to bear the weight of your identity. Relationships were not created for human beings in order to provide a sense of wholeness. You are already complete in Christ; relationships were given as a gift so you could experience love.

While my wife also had false things she was hoping the relationship would provide, my expectations did not give her space to develop awareness of her root. For my part, because I was in such need of my wife's approval and affection, I did take away her freedom to love me. It became an obligation, something she had to do well in order for her to feel relief. That's not a relationship of love. That is a relationship of necessity.

Just like exerting sustained pressure on an object will eventually deform it, existing in a relationship with the pressure to bear the burden of the weight of another's identity will deform the relationship. Ultimately, that happened for us, and without acknowledging it, we both gave up. My wife fully invested herself in our daughter, and for my sense of self I looked fully to my role in church. When that did not produce results, I looked to someone else entirely.

Relationships reveal our brokenness and how you focus on self. Because it is entered into with intended permanence, the marital relationship has been designed to force us to address the false self. Your inadequacies will be reflected back to you in the responses of your spouse. Your spouse knows you to a depth that no one else does, so they will rub up against your false sources of worth with great regularity. The anger, frustration, and unmet expectations tend to be symptoms of the false self encountering obstacles in getting what it wants. As mentioned in chapter 4, one response to this shame is to blame your spouse and heap more weight on their shoulders.

On the other hand, with the security of who you are in Christ, you can develop awareness of how you are trying to build yourself up, release your grip, and begin to love without concern to yourself. Putting another's needs alongside your own comes from not being rooted in self—this is selfless love.

What Love Is

Maybe the most famous exposition about love is the one penned by the apostle Paul in his letter to the Corinthian church. Because of its beauty and wisdom, this passage is a common part of weddings of both people who follow Christ and those who don't. Greeting cards and romantic valentines have the words tattooed on them. All of us are attracted to the idea of love.

But to reduce this passage to a commentary about romantic bliss or a standard of behavior is to completely miss its meaning. It is the picture of God's love that we get from Jesus, and is what we, when rooted in Christ, reflect to others.

Love is patient, love is kind. It does not envy, it does not boast, it is not proud. It does not dishonor others, it is not self-seeking, it is not easily angered, it keeps no record of wrongs. Love does not delight in evil but rejoices with the truth. It always protects, always trusts, always hopes, always perseveres. Love never fails.[5]

Paul is teaching what true love is, not for shame or behavior modification, but so you can judge your own fruit. Not displaying these qualities is symptomatic of a root that is disconnected from God.

- **Patience.** Impatience results when others are different from us, doing things differently, and you have trouble getting your way. This list starts with patience because love begins with acceptance. Love requires that you meet another person where they are, not where you want them to be

- **Kindness.** Being kind means having an eye for the needs of others. Displaying charity and generosity when it is not asked for and credit will not be given. Commonly, we love people the way we want to receive love, and kindness means developing an eye for what others need. In his book *The Inner Voice of Love*, Henri Nouwen wrote, "only when you know yourself as unconditionally loved – that is, fully received – by God can you give gratuitously."[6]

- **Not envious.** In many relationships, when one person receives praise or favor, the other feels slighted or marginalized. Without envy, love celebrates the successes and the victories of another without feeling like they are detracting from your own significance.

- **Not boastful.** One who boasts is looking to build themselves up in order to receive affirmation from another. In love, there is security in the truth about who you are. It is fine and good to give and receive praise, but doing it at the expense of another is not love.

- **Not prideful.** Pride is the root of the false self. As has been mentioned throughout this book, pride is an unhealthy inflation of your worth.

- **Honors.** Love holds others in high value. Recognizing the humanity and worth of all people regardless of socioeconomic class, occupation, etc.

- **Not self-seeking.** Love does not manipulate others to get what is desired. Jesus compares seeking exaltation for yourself to one who shows up at a dinner party and chooses for themselves the seat at the head of the table.[7] This is the effort to take and demand. Expecting to be honored originates with a focus on self.

- **Not easily angered.** Anger comes when you are kept from getting what you want or feel you need. It is a red alert, warning of an issue of identity in relationship. Always remember, righteous anger is directed at injustice, and more often than not our anger is an issue of wanting but not having.

- **Keeps no record of wrongs.** The reality of living in a broken world with imperfect people is that you will get hurt. People will disappoint you and not live up to expectations. Loving is giving another permission to potentially hurt you (not in any abusive way). Love does not hold these hurts over another's head, but rather forgives liberally because you have been fully forgiven.

- **Truthful.** Love is not indulgence. Love does not mean redefining truth so that others can be happy. There are boundaries and responsibilities that make freedom possible. Loving others means rejoicing in the truth, speaking it gently. Compassion without truth will not lead to change.

- **Love never fails.** Love is not a whim. As you love others, you make the effort to know and be known by them. Love is entered into with intentionality, and it always protects, trusts, hopes, and perseveres. It is not possible to truly love without knowing another.

This is not a formula. Jesus demonstrated these qualities of love so we could know how God loves us. This list shows you the outward expression of an identity that is satisfied in the truth of who you are and who God is. Love does not seek what is best for self, love seeks what is best for the other.

As my daughter was getting older and developing relationships at school, we had multiple conversations about what friendship is. In a culture that increasingly looks out for number one, it has become harder to know what being a friend and receiving friendship looks like. Here is the definition that I gave her based on the biblical idea of love: *a friend wants what's best for you even when it's not what's best for them.* Inversely, you will want what's best for your friends even when it is not best for you.

There is no fear in loving this way because another person's success or anger does not change who you are in Christ. So, like the four friends who loved their disabled brother, out of our love will come compassion, service, and the ability to tell another the truth. These are the relational fruit of being rooted in Christ.

None of us will display love perfectly. Now we only see a reflection of love. It is tainted by the battle of selves. The picture of love becomes clearer as you become your truer self. When you stand before Christ, then you will know love fully.[8]

Engaging In Love

In order to love someone fully, you must get into their experience and know them. Showing compassion means to suffer with another person. Being compassionate is the true definition of selflessly laying down your life for another.[9]

This is why telling someone to 'just stop' worrying, 'have more faith,' or to 'try harder' to not be a people pleaser is not effective. In and of itself, saying things like that is not a loving response because it places emphasis on self-effort, and when that fails, shame will be increased.

Everyone around me knew I was a people pleaser. I lived in awareness of my tendency. Some people in my life would often instruct me, *"You have got to just stop caring what people think about you."* After, we would laugh together about my antics, but when they left the room I would be confused and frustrated. Trying harder to act a new way only made things worse. When I'd get hurt by things that happened to me, I would feel the shame of failure and then look at God and wonder where He was in all of this.

One of my clients wanted to be less timid and was tired of being told to 'be bolder.' Without examining his root, words like those bore little fruit in his life. Change only began to happen when light was shed on what he felt was the value that timidity brought him. New behaviors come from a new root.

It is why another client, whom I've mentioned previously, who was consumed with her schedule and her busyness couldn't just stop saying yes to people's requests. She was walking around with the symptom of anxiety all the time because not only was she busy, she was failing at making good decisions. Attempting to change her decision-making process without touching its root only increased her frustration and shame.

Compassion is following words with presence—getting your hands dirty and joining another in developing awareness of their root. Do not confuse compassion with pity. Pity comes from looking down on others while a compassionate heart sees everyone in the same boat.

Similarly, compassion does not mean looking at people as a problem to be fixed; rather, they are someone to be joined with. When people are viewed as a problem to be fixed, they become an obligation, a burden, or an obstacle to some sort of success. It is only when we see the humanity in another person and how they were intended to live in the image of God that we can learn to be compassionate.

Of course, if you have a friend who is drinking too much or looking at porn or considering an affair, then you should tell them to stop. But, loving someone means that you will take the much harder step of helping them understand their root so it can be dug up and offered to Christ. Ministry in this way takes much more time and investment, but in the end it will have longer lasting results.

Truth be told, many church organizations don't to do a great job at this. When people are looked at as giving units, potential volunteers, future baptisms, etc., it reflects the mindset that people exist for a church's benefit. Once people are in the door and active, the organization moves on to the next group of newcomers. The truth that everyone we come in contact with is a person that God loves takes a backseat to other values.

In love we bear each other's burdens in order to lighten the load.[10] Just as Jesus did by being born into this world, love is demonstrated by moving toward others. Over and over in the New Testament, reminders are given to the original readers of how to love each other. Phrases like "honor", "serve", "build up", "encourage", "be devoted", and "bear with" speak to how each one of us is to lighten the load and enter the experience of others.

In one of the Apostle John's short letters, he says that whoever claims to be in the light but hates his brother is still in darkness.[11] The truth of this for your identity is that if you claim you are acting in love, but you are really using somebody else for your self-centered needs, you're only playing a part. You are fooling yourself with an unexamined root.

The Fruit of Acceptance

*Accept one another, then, just as Christ accepted you,
in order to bring praise to God.*[12]

As was noted previously in this chapter, loving someone begins with acceptance. Realizing that other people are broken differently than you are and also have different strengths and experiences is part of the process of acceptance. It is not an invitation to remain unchanged, but an awareness that where someone starts their path with Christ will be different from where they end.

The Bible calls this *grace*. When I began my spiritual journey of understanding identity in Christ, I was also in need of a new church community. My search took me to several churches while I was struggling to come to terms with what I had done, why I had done it, and was grieving everything that I had given up. I was living the Paschal Mystery.

Because of the size of the church that I had worked in, there had been some notoriety within the community concerning my departure. In the wake of this, there were many churches that I walked into where I felt unwelcome. People looked my way, shared whispers, and avoided talking to me. While I understood some of the initial reaction, the result was that my sense of failure was magnified by the isolation.

Yet, there was one place that was different. After many experiences, I had developed the strategy of being upfront when a church leader introduced themselves. Noticing that I was new, the pastor at this particular church came over to say hello. Once we had exchanged introductions and chit-chat, I told this man that I had been a pastor but I resigned because I had left my wife. Further, I told him that I was still trying to figure out what was going on with my marriage and if God could even love me after what I'd done. I finished with *"Am I welcome here?"* All I was looking for was a safe place to attend.

His reply stunned me when he said, *"Of course. Let's have lunch."* Here was somebody who was not afraid to be seen with someone who had failed. His grace and compassion started with acceptance.

Accepting others does not mean they first have to clean themselves up or make themselves look more like you do. That is conformity. Acceptance also means being aware that every one of us is broken differently. Each of us comes from different relational systems, have different temperaments, different circumstances and experiences, and so we each try to cover our shame in different ways. We cannot be scared of the sin of another, because all sin comes from a common root.

One of my close friends shared an experience that seems very common. He and his wife had been out of church for a while, and during a very tough season of life they decided to go back. On their first trip to a local church, when they entered, they were told to *"Put a smile on your faces, you are in the house of God."* Among the members, there was an attitude that for one to be accepted, they had to fit a certain mold. Yet, Jesus affirmed the attitude of acceptance as He attended a party filled with those who did not behave how the spiritual leaders wanted. Jesus told them, "It is not the healthy who need a doctor, but the sick."[13]

The standard of value that you hold to your life is how you measure the lives and works of others. If you are rooted in self, this prohibits acceptance.

Others will be viewed based on what they produce and how they perform.

Similarly, acceptance requires that we are aware and understand the differences in each other's strengths. Just as your acceptance by God leads to the fruit of your obedience, so will your acceptance of others give them the space and security to confront their own issues of identity. To me, this is why we are instructed to confess our sin to one another. Not as a way to compare each other spiritually and determine who the winner in the race of discipleship is, but as a way that we can show compassion to one another.

The typical accountability group that I have observed devolves into sharing the most external prayer requests because at some point, the group loses acceptance and becomes governed by fear. Having a bad week means that you've followed Jesus poorly and there is fear to report that back to the group. Frequently, shadows of your old nature creep in. Comparison forces you to put a mask on so people will not know where or who you really are. This partly comes from wanting Jesus to be seen as effective. It is rationalized that you are not being a good witness to people if your life does not look progressively better day by day.

The famous nineteenth century British preacher, Charles Spurgeon, said, "Appear to be what thou art, tear off thy masks. The church was never meant to be a masquerade." If Jesus is going to get credit for the change in your life, someone needs to see who you really are.

Being Differentiated

Typically, the picture of love we see in our culture is the pair of people who feel lost when they are apart. Yet, this picture of love is actually an example of two people who have defined themselves by their relationship. The term for this is *enmeshment*, a form of emotional dependence that is an imposter for love.

Being enmeshed can allow several negative patterns to develop. First, one person in the relationship can believe that everything is their fault. If they just performed better, then the other person would be happier or not angry. In this situation, one person is taking responsibility for the emotional state of both people in the relationship. An example that I have used in this book is the female client who believed if she could just be a 'Proverbs 31' wife, then her husband would notice her and realize her worth. Yet, the more she did, the less he cared. Her sense of self was tangled up with her husband's response.

Another pattern is the enabling of destructive behaviors. This is the spouse of the alcoholic who covers for missed days of work or abusive behavior because his or her sense of self is tied up in everything being perceived as OK. A couple I worked with wanted to be seen as 'good parents,' so they hid their son's drug habit and refused to allow him to experience any of the consequences. An enabler attempts to protect another from negative consequences.

In the enmeshed relationship, one person can lose their sense of self to the other. There is a drive to be what the other expects, and substitute that for acceptance. This may result in both people liking the same things and mimicking the same emotions. Sadly, I was enmeshed with my friends. In order to fit in, I dressed like others, claimed to enjoy the same activities, and responded to their insecurity with insecurities of my own. This is how relational systems replicate patterns.

Many couples that I have worked with misunderstand the idea of 'becoming one flesh' with enmeshment. In the act of becoming one flesh, many couples lose their individuality and grab onto each other for a sense of being complete.

Yet, this biblical concept does not mean losing touch with your individuality; it is about becoming one in identity. Being one in Christ, both people will be compelled toward their true self. Neither is dependent upon the other for identity. Hence there is security to work out salvation without fear of being rejected. Each spouse can serve the other without feeling demeaned in worth or tread upon. This truth is the foundation of Paul's writing to not "be yoked together with unbelievers."[14] Conflict will result when the person outside of Christ has nowhere else to look for identity but to the relationship.

What Love Does

"A new command I give you: Love one another. As I have loved you, so you must love one another. By this everyone will know that you are my disciples, if you love one another."[15]

Love speaks louder than words. Our love for God will serve as a deep pool from which love for others will spring. Not that we should force ourselves to act in a certain way. When those who are not following Christ see our love for one another, they should at once know that our following of Christ is the source.

How we treat each other should be so selfless that it stands in stark contrast to the brokenness and self-centeredness of the world. All of us are marked by the Spirit that helps to perfect our faith, and proof of that faith is the love we demonstrate. In describing the relationship between actions and faith, James wrote that he would show his faith by what he did.[16]

Who you are is not defined by what you do; rather what you do is defined by whose you are.

As you live in the middle of the spiritual desert, your loving treatment, your compassion, your ability to extend grace will communicate to a world that is thirsting for acceptance, meaning, and security. This is how people without the Spirit can come to know spiritual truths. They will see them on display through your demonstration of Christ's love to others. There is power in love.

This is the fruit of identity.

Gain Perspective

- Place yourself in the story of the men carrying their friend to Jesus. How do you feel when you see the crowd?

- Describe a time when loving someone felt overwhelming.

- Explain why compassion is difficult.

- Who needs your compassionate response? What is the first step you can take to offer it?

- In what way have you been treated like an object to support another's identity?

- What relational symptom do you most experience – anxiety, anger, disappointment, fear, or other? What is the source of this feeling?

- Think of your closest relationship (i.e. spouse, sibling, boy/girlfriend, best friend). How does this relationship reveal your passion for self?

- What is tough for you to accept in other people?

12

Living Your Mission

What is your purpose?

There is a growing trend in present-day Christian spirituality in which people are rejecting or leaving the church in order to follow Jesus on their own. Reasons given tend to be that leaders have failed or other followers have disappointed or hurt them. Because of the pain inflicted on them by others' failures, more and more people are seeking refuge by avoiding gathering with others altogether.

The church, like any system or organization, is made up of broken people who are each living their faith imperfectly. I will admit to struggling at various points with this cynicism as well. Over my time attending and leading in churches, I have been used for the gain of others and then discarded seemingly without thought. Each time this has happened, it's like a fresh wound. It seems like it would be very easy to shrug my shoulders, grab my wife by the hand, and not look back.

There is an unfortunate problem with this attitude. Each of us who follow Jesus has been called into a social, or communal, identity.[1] In Christ we are to be unified in purpose, desire, and source of significance. Following Him in our individualistic culture where everyone is compelled to do their own thing, we are becoming dissociated from our identity as a community of believers.

In John's short first letter, he addressed the issue by saying that when we walk in the light—meaning that our identity is rooted in the image of God—then we do so together.[2] When our life is surrendered to the truth, then "fellowship with one another" is the natural mode of expression. In the last chapter, we talked about how each of us is to demonstrate love for one another, but John's teaching takes it one step further. The term fellowship refers to something that is shared in common or to be joined together. For disciples, it speaks to the common source of definition and the resulting purpose that is shared among those who believe.

The book of Acts, which the doctor Luke wrote as a follow up to his self-named gospel about Jesus, is the story about the beginning and spread of the church after Jesus' ascension into heaven. Within the story, there is a short passage that gives a picture as to how those who were living in Christ acted towards one another. It begins with the phrase that "all the believers were one in heart and mind."[3] It is easy to gloss over this phrase, but every action of the early church has to be understood through this lens. Following Christ was not done in isolation.

With the heart being the source of worth and significance, the early church could function unified in their identity as the community of Christ. This caused them to also be one in thought about their purpose and how they related to the world around them. Among those who were part of the community, there was no one in need because what affected one had an effect on all. It was impossible to ignore the needs of another.

They were one.

Interconnected

In the final week of His life, Jesus spent a great deal of time focusing the disciples on the reality of what was about to happen to

Him and how it would impact them. Just before He was arrested, Jesus took time to pray first for Himself, then for His disciples, and finally for you and me, the recipients of their message.

As a model for the way that we are to exist with one another, Jesus spoke of His own relationship with the Father. His prayer was that those who follow Him "may be one as we are one."[4]

Like the Israelites, who gradually allowed the Law given by God to define them, we allow things other than Christ to define our communities. So, when theology defines our community, the result is denominational division. When certain type of worship music defines a group, there are church splits. It can be something as simple as how to raise kids that steals unity. All the way on the other end of the spectrum, it can be race or politics.

Regardless of the era, people are people and the apostle Paul had to confront divisions in the church, differing motivations, and perceived differences in value among those who composed the early churches he founded. In his letters to the church in Rome and Corinth, Paul did this by likening the group of Christ followers to a physical body.

Your body is very complex, formed from many different organs arranged in systems that each have a specific, vital purpose. While each system has its individual job, all work together to support the life of the whole. When a part is unhealthy or missing, then the body either cannot function or will not function up to its potential. So it is with the community of believers.[5]

By likening the community of Christ followers to a body, Paul was able to illustrate several points about how each of us relates to the other.

- *You cannot stop being part of the community.* Because of your identity in Christ, you were made to live in connection with other Christ followers.[6] If the hand decided to leave the rest of the body, it would soon wither and die. Your corresponding social identity is not something you can dismiss because you do not like your place or the people to whom you are connected. The way you have been designed, the experiences you bring into the gathering of followers, your temperament, your skills—everything—are what enable the body of Christ to function the way it is intended.

- *Everyone cannot be the same in the community.* Significance does not come from your role. If you compare yourself to another and determine whether you belong or not based on similarities, then you are deceived. The entire body cannot be made of eyes![7] Celebrate the way your true self has been created. Be joyful about how you uniquely fit. Do not compare and resent another because they seem to have more visibility. Jesus has reserved special honor for those parts that people notice less.[8] Your significance is found in Christ, not in the perceived worth of what you bring to the body. Remember Brother Lawrence? He was the monk who is remembered to this day despite being relegated to making soup for the rest of the monetary.

- *You cannot pick and choose who is part of the community.* Differences are not supposed to divide you from another, nor do you get to say *"I don't need you"*[9] to another. This air of superiority comes from being rooted in self. Each follower of Christ belongs to all the others.[10] There is no one, yourself included, who is dispensable.[11]

Each person who has entered into Christ has a role and a place that was created uniquely for them by God. To not be part of that leaves a gaping hole in the body.

We are all interconnected. As our roots in the image of God grow, they intertwine with those of other believers creating strength and stability. What happens to you, and how you are—both good and bad—affects and impacts those around you.

The church is a relational system. Just like yeast that works its way through the whole batch of dough, your decisions and behaviors have influence on those in your relational circle. You have the ability to build up or tear down those whom you are connected.

You can spur others on toward Christ or you can be a stumbling block. Because you are interconnected with others, your decisions and behaviors—and the true or false root they are supporting—will resonate throughout the system.

Working It Out

The process of working out your salvation—*discipleship*—is coming to a better understanding of who your true self really is. That process happens in community. On your own, your perception will be skewed. Alone, your tendency will be to fall prey to the lies of the enemy about who you are and who you perceive God to be. The disciples were sent by Jesus out in pairs because when one falls or is attacked, the other will be there to pick them up.[12] In gathering with others rooted in Christ, you will be reminded of truth.

I have several friends who are counselors. While being a good counselor takes a lot of skill and resilience, what they each tell me about the essence of counseling is pretty simple. They listen and remind. Their ability to listen provides space for the counselee to process feelings and decisions. As the processing happens, the counselor reminds the person of the truth of who they are. Over time and experience, the truth seeps in.

This is what each member of the body of Christ is to offer to the other: listening and reminding. Helping one another to discover their root and internalize truth. It is a process that takes patience and practice to change one's mindset and walk in confident belief.

Experience quickly teaches us that none of us will be perfect in offering this support. Broken people create broken systems. Imperfect people are prone to respond imperfectly. One result is that there will be hurts and disappointments in the community. But these imperfections are exactly why it is necessary for each of us to be part of something larger as we work it out. How we wrestle with identity, extend forgiveness and grace, and offer love is done in community, not in its absence.

Fractures in a relationship are breaks in the interconnectedness of the body. Because you are not perfect, you will inevitably wrong someone. To wrong someone is to not treat them with love. Ignoring their humanity, treating them in a selfish way, and using them to support your sense of identity. At the moment it comes to your awareness, your response in Christ is to drop what you are doing and seek to heal the relationship.[13]

Similarly, when someone wrongs you, the response from your identity in Christ should be to establish a boundary and tell them.[14] Then there can be reconciliation, and the interconnectedness that is essential to healthy community can be restored.

Taking on such attitudes are necessary for unity. Being one with each other and belonging to each other comes from humility. By denying self you affirm and strengthen identity in Christ.

Maintaining interconnectedness and unity does not mean maintaining appearances. How a community responds to failure says a lot about where that people's identity is rooted. When someone fails, do not be quick to cut their tree down. Many churches discard someone who struggles because it conflicts with the image that is trying to be portrayed. Instead of compassion, the message is come back when you get it together. Our job as a spiritual community is to love one another, not make Christ look effective through perfect actions. While maintaining a careful eye on your own root, every effort should be made to restore the wounded person gently.[15]

One of my clients was surprised by her husband's demand for a divorce. As she grieved the loss of the life she'd hoped for, she turned to the leaders of her church for support and guidance. When it became clear to them that the marriage could not be saved because the husband had already made up his mind, the church also asked this woman to leave. Marriage was such a defining value that they could not tolerate someone who had experienced failure in theirs. Instead of seeing this circumstance as the soil God would use to strengthen her root, they saw it as a lack of faith and obedience. This energetic and tender woman, who was working so diligently to unearth her false root, had been cast aside by the community that was supposed to build her up. For her, this was a legitimate compounding of hurt, but through our work, she realized that their actions reflected an issue of misplaced identity rather than a failure of Jesus in her life. She soon found a church that embraced her warmly and showed her the compassion she needed to recover and thrive.

Belonging

There are two pressing questions that I hear a lot and seem to plague people in modern culture. The first of these is *"Where do I belong?"* Belonging is a concept that is related to the foundational desire for acceptance and security we are born with.

It is not a group of people that defines you. When your self is defined by a community, then your response will be to conform to the expectations of that group. Because you have been created with a desire to belong, there is the temptation to see fitting in as a substitute for belonging. By attempting to fit in, you are attempting to earn affirmation from the group.

Being defined by Christ comes with a corresponding place to belong. Immediately upon entering Christ, your citizenship— where you belong—transfers to heaven.[16] As you continue to walk this earth, your reflection of that citizenship is expressed in the church.

Without the need to conform to be part of this spiritual group, there can be a sense of community. This is the experience of belonging. *"Authentic community is the place where differences are absorbed into a common thirst for another way of life."*[17] Differences among us no longer have meaning because they are not of value to who we are.

Thus, Paul wrote that in Christ *"there is neither Jew nor Gentile, neither slave nor free, nor is there male and female, for you are all one in Christ Jesus."*[18] With these words he is not saying that there are no longer any differences among followers of Christ. Diversity brings interest and shows off the creativity of God. What is meant is that those differences are to no longer have any power. Everyone in Christ belongs and is on equal footing. As it is said in the Barnes quote above, these differences among us are absorbed.

Your Mission

The second question that consumes much of our thinking is *"Why am I here?"* This is the question of purpose. One of the unfortunate consequences of the false self pursuing wholeness apart from God is that purpose is stolen. With an absent God, purpose is no bigger than pursuing what will build the false sense of self up.

If you have ever seen a satellite image of land at night, it is easy to spot the cities for they are clusters of bright light. The larger the city is, the more intense the light. (Check it out for yourself by doing an internet search for "satellite images of cities at night.") Seeing the gobs of light can give you understanding of what Jesus meant when He told His disciples that "You are the light of the world. A town built on a hill cannot be hidden."[19] Herein also lies the key to your purpose.

In the day of Jesus, a city that was built on a hill would have been a source of protection for the community that surrounded it. In a time of attack, the walls would have provided safety. Looking up to the city would have been a source of hope and assurance.

Just like the city on the hill, the world is to be able to look to the spiritual community of Christ followers as a source of light and hope. The stronger the links among His followers are, the brighter the light that will be reflected. In Jesus' prayer for the oneness of those who would follow Him referred to earlier in the chapter, He gives reason for that unity. The unity of His body is to show the world that the Father sent Jesus and that He has undying love for them.[20] Your participation in the church, your experience of belonging is to be a demonstration to those who do not know God of His love for them. This is your mission.

The church gives the picture of God's healing power.

It is interesting that the church's gradual loss of influence in our culture has corresponded to a growing disunity in the body brought about by different groups seeking identity in different things beyond Christ. The church, of which you and I are a part, is not to be in competition with the world in an attempt to attract others by being bigger, more powerful or aligned with the right powers.

If Christ did not come to condemn the world[21], then His body should not condemn the world. If the church is to be a light to the world, then it should not reflect the values of culture.

The church should be in a loving mission to the world by faithfully administering God's grace in its many forms. Together and interconnected, we are to be servants of the world, following the example of the One in Whom our identity rests.

The community of believers has made and will make mistakes. That reality is a product of still being present in this broken world system.

But, aligned with Christ rather than worldly approval, we have the ability to offer repentance, in stark contrast to a world that is rooted in pride and perfection.

Collectively, as the body of Christ we are His image for the world to see. A world, remember, that cannot understand spiritual things without an example before them.

Together we become the image of goodness, grace, restoration, acceptance, and compassion. This is another reason that being in Christ is a group identity. Because we are in the process of being restored in the likeness of Christ, our personal imperfection will not give a full picture of who Jesus is. It is together, as we pick up those who fall, as we join people in their suffering, and as we live as those approved by Christ despite our performance, that the world gets a full picture of the love of Jesus.

What image of Christ are we presenting to those around us? If we appear to be serving a Savior that cannot be made happy, then that is not an offer of hope to people who are serving sources of identity that can never quench thirst. Such a savior stands in dissonance to Jesus' promises that in Him we would experience peace and rest.

Instead, offer the world the message that in Christ God is already pleased. It is not about what they do, it is about what Christ has done. In answering definitively and securely the questions of identity, Jesus has taken the pressure off their shoulders. This is a message that is novel and captivating. This is hope.

Attending a spiritual group or local church is not an act of obligation. Your participation is not a practice that is done for one hour on Saturday night or Sunday mornings. Gathering together, being one with others in spiritual community, is to be a regular expression of your life rooted in Christ.

Your life's mission that came as a package deal when you surrendered your identity to Christ is to be an agent of reconciliation.[22] Helping others to uproot their tree of lies and find their definition of self in the image of God is the mission, and the only thing that will last beyond this world.

Gain Perspective

- On a scale of 1 (low) to 10 (high), rate how important gathering with other followers of Christ is to your spirituality. What is the reason for your rating?

- Explain the implications of being *"one in heart and mind"* (Acts 4:32).

- How have you taken on the behaviors of others? Has this been healthy or unhealthy?

- Who has wronged you, and with the situation remaining unresolved? What obstacle is there to resolution?

- Who have you wronged, and with the situation remaining unresolved? What obstacle is there to seeking resolution?

- Where do you seek belonging?

- How can you live the mission described in this chapter?

13 | Working It Out

How do you respond to failure?

The symbolism of the day was not lost to me, nor was it lost on my counselor as we reflected on the past year together. This was a day of new life. I have been asked by the church that I was attending to provide the congregational welcome and do the announcements for Easter Sunday. Talking in front of people is something I am good at doing, so I was eager to contribute my abilities.

It had been just a smidge over a year since the Good Friday on which I experienced a very real death. At the time, my false self was at the beginning of its death. Now it was going to be Easter Sunday, the day that followers of Christ celebrate his resurrection from the dead and entrance into new life in His name, and I was going to stand before people as a new man. The people in attendance didn't know it; they just saw an energetic guy wearing a new shirt and a huge grin. Those who had walked the compassionate path with me knew: the pastor of the church, my counselor, my wife, and my small group of friends.

I had changed.

Over the course of the previous 12 months, I had wrestled with where my purpose was. As a way to contribute, yet not have to interact with many people, I had spent time on the set-up team at the church. At 5:30 in the morning, guys don't seem to have too much to say to each other as if they are setting out chairs and toys in kids' Sunday school rooms. But I could not help the nagging feeling that God was drawing me back in. This went against everything that I thought about God, and about working with people in a Christian leadership context. I just didn't think that it would be possible to teach or shepherd or provide counsel for anybody. My failure had separated me from that.

We have such a fear of failure. Not only does this fear purvey our culture, it is mirrored in the church. Rather than an opportunity to learn, failure becomes the way we define ourselves. To many church leaders, I was the failed pastor. Yet, it is in the realm of failure that God works His greatest miracles.

Failure Doesn't Define You

With good reason, David is often looked up to by people who read the Bible as a man who was after God's own heart. This was God's own description of how He saw David.[1] High praise from the One who picked him to be king of Israel. David, though, was not without sin. One of the incidents we are told about is his lust for and pursuit of another man's wife.

Not only did he commit adultery with Bathsheba, David had this woman's husband killed so that he could marry her. He might have gotten away with it in the eyes of man, but God knew. That is epic failure. David had turned his eyes from God and looked toward something else for wholeness. His act of defiance was the result of attempting to satisfy himself and cover his shame.

Even thought his root in the image of God had atrophied, it was still present. When confronted by the prophet Nathan about what he had done, David fell on his face in repentance.[2] Awareness from his spiritual community helped to restore David's root.

What cannot be overlooked is that the king who oversaw Israel's glory days, the man who is attributed more wisdom than anyone in the whole world and wealth such that leaders around the world came just to put their eyes on it, was the future son of David and Bathsheba. Apparently, in God's economy, those who fail greatly can still be used significantly.

This was not God condoning their sin, but the Paschal Mystery of new life coming from death. Failure did not define Dave. Rooted in His image, God saw David's true self.

About two years after my wife and I began the reconciliation process, which was the same time I began walking the journey of understanding my identity in Christ, I spoke at a conference for pastors that dealt with failure. It was called the Epic Fail Pastors' Conference. I was as shocked that it was a real thing as you probably are right now. I wasn't alone.

In a room of about 75 pastors, I got the chance to speak for 40 minutes about my failure and its origin. My life was on display as an example of the Paschal Mystery. These men and women who had failed in a variety of ways needed to be told that failure does not define them in the Kingdom of God.

It was a very powerful moment for me, with many of the pastors coming up and talking to me afterward about my failure compared to theirs and seeing hope. At the end of the three days, one of the attendees gave me a ride to the airport. In our hour in the car together, he started our conversation off by saying, *"I want to tell you some things that no other living person knows."* That got my attention! He felt trust because of the weakness and vulnerability I had put on display.

God will do the same thing with you as you work on your identity in Christ. Whatever actions—large or small—you have pursued in your quest to find wholeness apart from Him are forgiven and do not change the truth about who you are. Others will be drawn to your experience.

Being Influential

True influence comes not from having everything all put together, but from allowing people to see that you don't. In this they will see the extent of your reliance on Jesus and how he is your strength. Living with the knowledge that Jesus already approves of who you are will take the weight off your shoulders.

When we read the Bible, our tendency is to look at the stories as examples of heroes who were strong in the Lord. But maybe the next time you read, change your lens to see these as people who feel the same things you do, with the same fears, temptations, hopes, and expectations. There is nothing new under the sun[3], and the lies you believe about yourself and ways you are tempted to fulfill your identity are the same as for these people in the Bible. All of them were human.

Even when we read about David going against the giant, that story has become the false narrative about the underdog beating the big bully. Instead, it is about the failure of a nation to live in their God-given identity. Israel had lost its trust for the God who had called them. It took a boy, with a heart aligned with God, to step forward. It wasn't David defeating Goliath that was heroic, it was that he was firmly living in his identity as image bearer of God. The strength of David was the trust that God would keep His explicit promise of protection to His nation.

The Bible is the story of a God who created humanity and created people to function in connection to Him. Page after page, humanity's belief of the Lie is evident as people pursue wholeness apart from him. God's response is to pursue at literally all costs.

I am still working out my salvation. For each of us, that will be a lifelong process. There are still things that are tough. In my marriage, I still struggle against keeping my wife happy in order to maintain peace. My mindset as a husband, father, business owner, speaker, friend, and disciple must constantly be that people's response to me does not define my worth.

When the enemy tempts you that you are alone in whatever you're dealing with, take comfort in my experience. When I tell people about identity, and in particular about my tendency to place my value in what people think of me, inevitably I hear the response *"Me too."* Or when I tell people about my marriage struggles and disappointments, rather than being a turn-off, doors of conversation get opened. This has happened so many times; I wish I had been opened to this lesson so much sooner.

It is not the healthy that need a doctor, it is the sick. When you are vulnerable and trust the security of who you are, sharing opens the door for others who are sick to see themselves clearly and grasp onto the hope that you have.

Jesus asked a man sitting by a pool in Jerusalem, *"Do you want to get well?"*[4] This man had grasped onto his handicap as a way to define himself. Even though he was literally sitting next to a pool that could heal him, he was comfortable and knew what to expect in his situation. He could say that he wanted to get better, make excuses, and avoid taking a step. As they parted, Jesus told the man to stop sinning—meaning, stop finding your wholeness apart from God.

This man had been paralyzed for thirty-eight years and was up against a wall of lies that he could not break through. That is the truth about the barriers that we encounter in our hearts when we begin to examine our identity. You can't break through them with force; you can't tunnel under them. Walls must be deconstructed brick by brick. That's a slower type of growth than we hope for in our fast-paced, instantaneous results-oriented culture. But it is this growth that is modeled in nature. Before the stalk of the plant breaks through the soil, the root has already started to develop. Root development leads to plant development.

Do you want to get well?

Do you want freedom? Are you ready for peace and rest? There are going to be obstacles and there are going to be times when you try to do the same things you used to do. Sometimes, discipleship is going to involve taking two steps backwards. Sometimes, you're going to look in the mirror and feel like you haven't made any progress at all. That is normal. God does not run from your failure.

The truth is that your root might be developing and the outward expression has not materialized yet.

Remember, trees bear their fruit in season.

Gain Perspective

I hope that this book and the dozens of questions at the end of each chapter have helped you take the first steps towards root development. For more companion resources to this book, visit http://treeoflies.com to gain further perspective on identity and its impact on decisions, behaviors, and relationships.

Also, you can find a series of seven videos along with accompanying worksheets at **http://treeoflies.com/discover**. These complementary resources will help you develop disciplines and identify areas that you are allowing to define your sense of self.

I discovered my passion and purpose in life through this process. I want to help people following Christ take steps into freedom by walking with them as they develop awareness of who they are in Christ. It is what compelled me to write this book and what gets me out of bed each morning.

I pray for the same transformation for you in your life in Christ.

Appendix A

Discovering Your Root

I am so glad that you read *Tree of Lies*. My passion is to help you *gain perspective* of your identity so that you can *live well*. In order to join you in developing your root in Christ, I have created a series of sixteen coaching videos available at http://DiscoveringYourRoot. com. These resources will guide you in:

- Setting spiritual goals.

- Pursuing God according to your design.

- Understanding your response to shame.

- Defining relational patterns.

- Developing a healthy rhythm of life.

- Managing your busyness.

- Identifying core lies.

- Creating a new mindset.

- Energizing your discipleship.

- Reducing conflict.

- Pursuing your purpose.

- Pruning unhealthy behaviors and relationships.

- And much more.

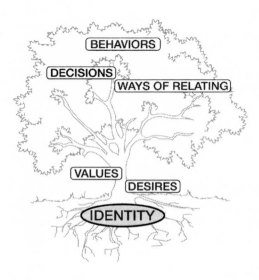

Go to http://DiscoveringYourRoot.com and continue to build momentum in transforming your decisions, behaviors, and relationships.

Appendix B

Developing an Identity Statement in Christ

Creating a statement about who you are in Christ can be a powerful exercise in realizing the truth about how God sees you. It also builds up the storehouse of truth you have to answer the lies about your identity that the enemy will throw at you. As you craft your statement of identity, it will serve as a vision of your true self—who God intended you to be when He created you.

Visit http://treeoflies.com/identity to read my identity statement that I created in the days after admitting to my counselor that I was empty and did not think God understood (see the opening paragraph of chapter 1).

Also included at that page is a video to guide you in the process of forming your statement and a list of dozens of scriptures to get you started in your examination of the truth of who you are.

Appendix C

31 Days of Identity Devotions

All of us need encouragement as we follow Christ. Particularly as you learn new ways to think and relate, having someone in your corner can keep you taking the next step.

I'd be honored to provide that encouragement for you. For that reason, I have set up 31 days of identity devotions to be delivered to your email inbox.

Simply go to http://treeoflies.com/31days to sign up and then set aside a few undistracted minutes each day to savor them.

Each day will include a scripture, short teaching or story related to identity, and a question or two that you can use as you start the day, rest on a lunch break, or begin an end of the day examen.

Selected Bibliography

Allen, Diogenes. *Spiritual Theology*. Cambridge, MA: Cowley Publications. 1997.

Au, Wilkie, and Noreen Cannon. *Urgings of the Heart*. Mahwah, NJ: Paulist Press. 1995.

Bailey, Kenneth E. *The Cross & the Prodigal*. Downers Grove, IL: IVP Books. 2005.

Barnes, M. Craig. *Sacred Thirst*. Grand Rapids, MI: Zondervan. 2001.

Barnes, M. Craig. *When God Interrupts*. Downers Grove, IL: InterVarsity Press. 1996.

Barnes, M. Craig. *Yearning*. Downers Grove, IL: InterVarsity Press. 1991.

Benner, David G. *The Gift of Being Yourself*. Downers Grove, IL: IVP Books. 2004.

Benner, David G. *Sacred Companions*. Downers Grove, IL: IVP Books. 2002.

Benner, David G. *Surrender to Love*. Downers Grove, IL: IVP Books. 2003.

Brown, Brene. *The Gifts of Imperfection*. Center City, MN: Hazelden. 2010.

Brown, Brene. *I Thought It Was Just Me*. New York, NY: Gotham Books. 2007.

Chan, Simon. *Spiritual Theology*. Downers Grove, IL: IVP Academic. 1998.

Cloud, Dr. Henry. *Changes That Heal*. Grand Rapids, MI: Zondervan. 1992.

Cloud, Dr. Henry. *Necessary Endings*. New York, NY: Harper Business. 2010.

Crabb, Larry. *The Pressure's Off*. Colorado Springs, CO: Waterbrook Press. 2002.

Crabb, Larry. *Shattered Dreams*. Colorado Springs, CO: Waterbrook Press. 2001.

Friedman, Edwin H. *Generation to Generation*. New York, NY: The Guilford Press. 1985.

Hagberg, Janet O., and Robert A. Guelich. *The Critical Journey*. Salem, WI: Sheffield Publishing. 2005.

Hougen, Judith. *Transformed into Fire*. Grand Rapids, MI: Kregel Publishers. 2002.

Idleman, Kyle. *Not a Fan*. Grand Rapids, MI: Zondervan. 2011.

Keating, Thomas. *Open Mind, Open Heart*. New York, NY: Continuum. 1999.

Keller, Timothy. *Prodigal God*. New York, NY: Dutton. 2008.

Lawrence, Bro. The Practice of the Presence of God. New

Kensington, PA: Whitaker House. 1982.

Leman, Dr. Kevin. *The Birth Order Book*. Old Tappan, NJ: Fleming H. Revell Company. 1985.

Lovelace, Richard F. *Renewal as a Way of Life*. Downers Grove, IL: InterVarsity Press. 1985.

Manning, Brennan. *Ruthless Trust*. New York, NY: HarperOne. 2000.

McGee, Robert S. *The Search for Significance*. Nashville, TN: Thomas Nelson. 2003.

McGoldrick, Monica, and Randy Gerson. *Genograms in Family Assessment*. New York, NY: W. W. Norton & Company. 1985.

Moon, Gary W. *Homesick for Eden*. LifeSprings Resources. 1996.

Mulholland Jr., M. Robert. *The Deeper Journey*. Downers Grove, IL: IVP Books. 2006.

Mulholland Jr., M. Robert. *Invitation to a Journey*. Downers Grove, IL: IVP Books. 1993.

Nouwen, Henri J. M. *The Return of the Prodigal Son*. New York, NY: Image Books. 1994.

Pennington, M. Basil. *True Self, False Self*. New York, NY: The Crossroad Publishing Co. 2000.

Rolheiser, Ronald. *The Holy Longing*. New York, NY: Doubleday. 1999.

Rolheiser, Ronald. *The Shattered Lantern*. New York, NY: The Crossroad Publishing Co. 2001.

Scarf, Maggie. *Intimate Worlds*. New York, NY: Random House. 1995.

Scazzero, Peter. *Emotionally Healthy Spirituality*. Nashville, TN:

Thomas Nelson. 2006.

Thrall, Bill, Bruce McNicol, and John Lynch. *TrueFaced*. Colorado Springs, CO: NavPress. 2004.

Webber, Robert E. *The Divine Embrace*. Grand Rapids, MI: Baker Books. 2006.

Willard, Dallas. *Renovation of the Heart*. Colorado Springs, CO: NavPress. 2002.

Yancey, Philip. *Vanishing Grace*. Grand Rapids, MI: Zondervan. 2014.

Acknowledgements

Writing a book is a difficult and sometimes all-consuming process. Because of that, it is not something that can be done alone. Many people have impacted me and shaped the truths that are contained in this book. If you have been a friend to me then know that you are part of this project.

In particular, I'd like to thank the following people for what they directly contributed to this book becoming a reality:

- Missy and Sarah Perkins. Thank you for the space you gave me and the cheers of encouragement. You both have been patient listening to me talk for three years about the book I'm writing. I hope you see Christ working in me.

- Ronnie Mesa. Lots of the ideas in this book got sharpened in your garage. Thank you for your friendship and generosity. My logo and the tree graphics in this book are spectacular.

- Debbie Miller. Without your spiritual guidance, I would not have been able to write this book. Thank you for your wisdom, counsel, and friendship.

- Joe McLeod. You were the first to read this book all the way through, and there were times that your encouragement propelled me to write the next chapter. Thank you for all the time you spent reading and providing insights. They were invaluable.

- Brian Miller. Throughout this process, as I was filled with doubts and questions, you kept me focused on getting this book written for the right reasons. Thank you for being steadfast and in my corner.

- Kary Oberbrunner. The coaching that you have provided helped me overcome my "mindfield." Thank you for all the energy you put into making your coaching life changing.

- Precy Larkins. This book is better and more readable because of your editing. Thank you for enduring my continual misuse of commas and tendency to type "in" instead of "and."

- Dad and Mom. No one in my life is more supportive than the two of you. Thank you for encouraging me and giving me a foundation to build on. Both of you are amazing.

- Finally, thank you to the group of people who provided funding to help me get this project done: Kathryn Angulo, Debra Cross, Zac Dodson, Terry Hoehn, Dean Hutchinson, Sharon Latran, Barry Mais, Joe McLeod, Elaine Packard, Dave Pearce, Paul Pletcher, Amy Sinico, and Karen Willis.

Contacting Scott

Perkins

Gain Perspective • Live Well

Choosing the right speaker for your church or organization can be a daunting task. With relevant content, engaging personality, wealth of experience, and personal follow-up, Scott Perkins is the perfect choice for a variety of contexts.

Contact Scott when you are planning your next:

- Workshop or seminar
- Church guest speaker

- Weekend retreat
- Lunch and Learn
- Conference

Scott has the flexibility to provide talks on the topic you need or work with you to tailor a message specifically for your church or organization.

Email: **Scott@PerkinsPerspectives.com**

Endnotes

Chapter 1 – Burning Out

[1] James 4:1-2

[2] 2 Corinthians 12:7

[3] Romans 7:22-23

[4] Romans 8:28

[5] John 8:32, 36

[6] Matthew 11:28

[7] Luke 10:38-42

[8] https://barna.org/research/leaders-pastor

[9] Matthew 12:33

[10] Isaiah 64:6

Chapter 2 – The Tree of Life

[1] Genesis 1:27

[2] Genesis 1:28

[3] Genesis 2:25

4 Brown, Brene. *The Gifts of Imperfection*. Center City, MN: Hazelden. 2010.

5 Genesis 2:23

6 Genesis 2:20

7 Genesis 17:1-2

8 Exodus 6:7

9 1 Samuel 8:7

10 Colossians 1:15

11 John 14:6

12 Pennington, M. Basil. *True Self, False Self*. New York, NY: The Crossroad Publishing Company. 2000. p. 32

13 Genesis 1:26

14 Acts 17:21

15 Acts 17:28

16 Colossians 2:9-10a

17 Acts 5:41

18 Luke 6:44

Chapter 3 – The Root of the Problem

1 Mark 10:17

2 Mark 10:22

3 Hougen, Judith. *Transformed into Fire*. Grand Rapids, MI: Kregel Publications. 2002. p. 59

4 John 4:4-17

5 Genesis 2:17

6 Benner, David. *The Gift of Being Yourself*. Downers Grove, IL: IVP Books. 2004. p. 75

7 Genesis 3:6

[8] Genesis 3:16a

[9] Genesis 3:16b

[10] Genesis 3:7-8

[11] Jeremiah 2:13

[12] Galatians 5:19-21

[13] Matthew 7:17-18

[14] Proverbs 22:6

[15] Luke 13:8

[16] John 2:25

[17] Hagberg, Janet O. and Robert A. Guelich. *The Critical Journey*. Salem, WI: Sheffield Publishing. 2005. p. 17

Chapter 4 – The Cover Up

[1] 2 Corinthians 10:12

[2] Romans 13:14

[3] Genesis 3:6

[4] Genesis 3:7-13

[5] Hougen, Judith. *Transformed into Fire*. Grand Rapids, MI: Kregel Publications. 2002.

[6] Luke 9:54

[7] Judges 2:10-11 for one instance

[8] Romans 7:15

[9] 2 Corinthians 12:9

Chapter 5 – Core Lies

[1] Pennington, M. Basil. *True Self, False Self*. New York, NY: The Crossroad Publishing Company. 2000. p. 28

[2] Pennington, M. Basil. *True Self, False Self*. New York, NY: The Crossroad Publishing Company. 2000. p. 30

[3] Scarf, Maggie. *Intimate Worlds*. New York, NY: Random House. 1995. p. xxxiv

[4] Leman, Dr. Kevin. *The Birth Order Book*. Old Tappan, NJ: Fleming H. Revell Co. 1984.

[5] Genesis 5:3

[6] Scarf, Maggie. *Intimate Worlds*. New York, NY: Random House. 1995. p. 44

[7] Genesis 25:28

[8] Luke 14:26

[9] Ephesians 1:5

[10] Barnes, M. Craig. *When God Interrupts*. Downers Grove, IL: InterVarsity Press. 1996. p. 128

[11] Colossians 3:10

[12] Matthew 25:20, 22

[13] Luke 15:11-32

[14] Romans 12:2

[15] 2 Corinthians 4:18; Hebrews 12:2

[16] John 8:32

Chapter 6 – God's Surprising Response to Brokenness

[1] Genesis 3:9

[2] Genesis 17:22

[3] God's invitation to Abraham to *"walk before me and be perfect"* is an invitation to dwell in His presence. The invitation enables Abraham to derive his sense of self from God. It is not an injunction to perform better.

[4] Mark 16:7

[5] Luke 24:34; 1 Corinthians 15:5

[6] John 21

[7] John 1:14

[8] Colossians 1:21

[9] Matthew 22:19-21

[10] Genesis 22

[11] Colossians 1:22

[12] John 21:3

[13] John 21:6

[14] John 21:15

[15] Matthew 26:33

[16] John 14:8

[17] John 14:9

[18] 1 Corinthians 2:14

[19] Matthew 28:20

[20] John 20:31

[21] Matthew 7:21-23

[22] James 4:8

[23] Ephesians 2:10

[24] 1 Kings 19

[25] 1 Corinthians 10:31

[26] Arnold, J. Heinrich. *Discipleship*. Robertsbridge, East Sussex: Plough Publishing. 1994.

[27] Benner, Dr. David. *Sacred Companions*. Downers Grove, IL: IVP Books. 2002.

Chapter 7 – The Desert Life

[1] Romans 1:21-25

[2] Matthew 19:27

3 Luke 3:22

4 The passage being referenced is Luke 4:1-13, although the same encounter is recorded in Matthew 4:1-11 and Mark 1:12-13

5 John 14:6; 1 Peter 2:22

6 John 4:1-42

7 Psalm 1:1-3

8 Mulholland Jr., M. Robert. *Shaped By the Word*. Nashville, TN: The Upper Room. 1985.

9 Romans 12:2

10 Hebrews 11:1

11 2 Corinthians 2:15

12 Thrall, Bill, Bruce McNicol, and John Lynch. *TrueFaced*. Colorado Springs, CO: NavPress. 2004.

13 Romans 8:5

14 Philippians 3:19

15 Colossians 3:2

16 Matthew 10:29

17 Matthew 10:30

18 2 Corinthians 5:21

19 Colossians 2:10

20 Psalm 103:12

21 Hebrews 4:15

22 John 15:3

23 Hebrews 12:2

24 John 21:21

Chapter 8 – Planting a New Root

[1] Matthew 16:16

[2] Matthew 16:24

[3] 1 John 1:10

[4] 2 Corinthians 10:12

[5] John 10:28

[6] Hebrews 13:5

[7] Luke 18:9-14

[8] 2 Corinthians 12:10

[9] 1 Corinthians 11:1

[10] Galatians 5:17

[11] Acts 7:58

[12] 1 Corinthians 15:9

[13] Ephesians 3:8

[14] 1 Timothy 1:15

[15] Hebrews 11:1

[16] Jeremiah 17:9

[17] Matthew 15:17-20

[18] Genesis 25:34

[19] Proverbs 4:23

[20] Benner, Dr. David. *Desiring God's Will*. Downers Grove, IL: IVP Books. 2005. p. 14

Chapter 9 – The Mystery of Faith

[1] Benner, Dr. David. *Soulful Spirituality*. Grand Rapids, MI. Brazos Press. 2011. p. 63

[2] Rolheiser, Ronald. *The Holy Longing*. New York, NY: Doubleday. 1999. p. 146

[3] Matthew 16:24

[4] Matthew 11:30

[5] Genesis 32:25

[6] 2 Corinthians 12:7

[7] Romans 8:28-29

[8] Exodus 12

[9] 1 Timothy 3:16

[10] Romans 5:3-5

[11] 1 Samuel 16:1

[12] Luke 19:8

[13] Rolheiser, Ronald. *The Holy Longing*. New York, NY: Doubleday. 1999. p. 164

[14] Genesis 19:26

[15] Rolheiser, Ronald. *The Holy Longing*. New York, NY: Doubleday. 1999. p. 157

[16] Benner, Dr. David. *Desiring God's Will*. Downers Grove, IL: IVP Books. 2005 p. 109

[17] Galatians 6:2

[18] John 12:24

Chapter 10 – Following Jesus

[1] Matthew 6:5, 15 for instance

[2] Matthew 16:24

[3] Luke 9:23

[4] Mark 7:18-23

[5] 1 Corintians 3:7-9

[6] Scazzaro, Peter. *Emotionally Healthy Spirituality*. Nashville, TN: Thomas Nelson. 2006.

7 Exodus 34:14

8 Luke 8:11-15

9 Mulholland Jr., M. Robert. *Invitation to a Journey.* Downers Grove, IL: IVP Books. 1993.

10 Foster's *Celebration of Discipline*, Willard's *The Spirit of the Disciplines*, and Whitney's *Spiritual Disciplines for the Christian Life* are three that I would recommend.

11 Matthew 14:13; 26:36; Mark 1:35 among others

12 James 5:16

13 Matthew 6:12

14 Matthew 18:21-35

15 Philippians 4:8

16 Matthew 6:1-4

17 Proverbs 19:17

18 Brown, Stuart. *Play.* New York, NY: Avery. 2009.

19 Romans 1:20

20 Psalm 119:11

21 Cloud, Dr. Henry. *Necessary Endings.* New York, NY: Harper-Collins. 2010. p. 15-16

22 Matthew 22:2

23 Matthew 25:21

Chapter 11 – Not Meant to Be Alone

1 Mark 2:3-5

2 1 John 3:16

3 2 Corinthians 5:18

4 Matthew 23:25-28

5 1 Corinthians 13:4-8a

[6] Nouwen, Henri J. M. *The Inner Voice of Love*. New York, NY: Doubleday. 1996. p. 65

[7] Luke 14:7-11

[8] 1 Corinthians 13:12

[9] John 15:13

[10] Galatians 6:2

[11] 1 John 2:9

[12] Romans 15:7

[13] Matthew 9:12

[14] 2 Corinthians 6:14

[15] John 13:34-35

[16] James 2:18

Chapter 12 – Living Your Mission

[1] Malina, Bruce J. and John J. Pilch. *Social-Science Commentary on the Letters of Paul*. Minneapolis, MN: Fortress Press. p. 31

[2] 1 John 1:7

[3] Acts 4:32a

[4] John 17:21, 22

[5] Romans 12:4-5

[6] 1 Corinthians 12:15,16

[7] 1 Corinthians 12:17-19

[8] 1 Corinthians 12:23

[9] 1 Corinthians 12:21

[10] Romans 12:5

[11] 1 Corinthians 12:22

[12] Ecclesiastes 4:10

[13] Matthew 5:23-24

[14] Luke 17:3

[15] Galatians 6:1

[16] Philippians 3:20

[17] Barnes, M. Craig. *Sacred Thirst*. Grand Rapids, MI: Zonder-van. 2001.
p. 48

[18] Galatians 3:28

[19] Matthew 5:14

[20] John 17:23b

[21] John 3:17

[22] 2 Corinthians 5:18

Chapter 13 – Working It Out

[1] 1 Samuel 13:14

[2] 2 Samuel 12:13

[3] Ecclesiastes 1:9

[4] John 5:6

CPSIA information can be obtained at www.ICGtesting.com
Printed in the USA
LVOW08s0142080716

495261LV00004B/7/P